W9-BSF-224

Nations and Peoples

Belgium

Belgium

MARGOT LYON

with 28 illustrations and 4 maps

WALKER AND COMPANY
NEW YORK

To Richard and Jerry

ISBN 0–8027–2122–2

Library of Congress Catalog Card Number: 68–13971

First published in the United States of America in 1971 by the Walker Publishing Company, Inc.

Printed in Great Britain by Cox & Wyman Ltd,
London, Fakenham and Reading

Contents

1   Medieval riches

THE TWENTY-SEVENTH OF JULY, 1950: a hot summer afternoon. From the centre of Brussels a crowd several thousand strong marches towards the Palace of Laeken, to protest against the return of King Leopold III, just back after six years of exile. The demonstrators violently reject Leopold. But they are not republicans: they are willing and eager to accept his son Baudouin in his place. Still less are they by nature revolutionaries. Most of them are Socialists, and Belgian Socialism is remarkable for its solid bourgeois values. More paradoxically still, they are led by Paul-Henri Spaak, the world's best-known and most respected Belgian, fresh from international triumphs as first president of the United Nations' Assembly, first chairman of OEEC, first president of the Assembly of the Council of Europe. What is he doing there? What are they all doing?

Outside the palace gates the marchers confront a hostile mass of King Leopold's supporters, most of them from Belgium's Catholic party – which draws its main strength from the small Flemish towns of northern Belgium, as the Socialist party does from the great industrial cities of the Walloon south. Mounted police stand by. There is noise and heat and excitement, but characteristically there is no bloodshed. Finally, the crowds disperse.

Certainly, that is not the end. It could not be: the affair has roots that go back further than the years of the King's exile, deep into Belgium's history. Confronting each other at Laeken were not merely the supporters and opponents of King Leopold, but the two faces of Belgium: Catholics and anti-clericals, Flemish tradition and French radicalism, country and town, north and south, agriculture

7

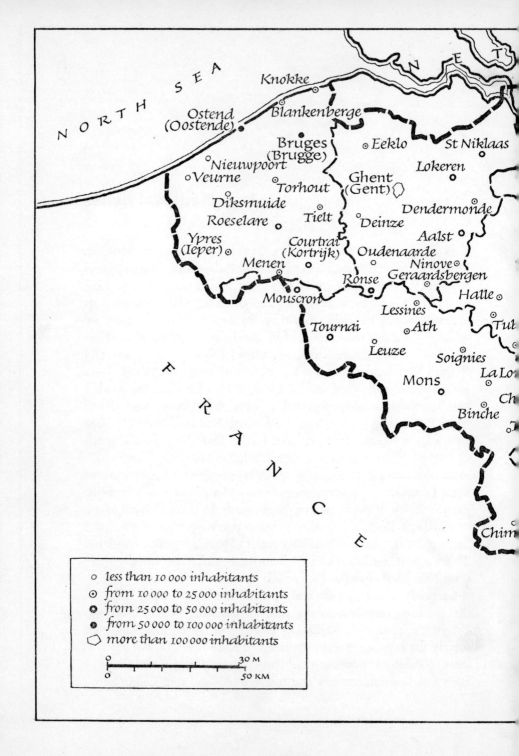

NORTH SEA

N E T

Knokke

Ostend
(Oostende)

Blankenberge

Bruges
(Brugge)

Eeklo

St Niklaas

Nieuwpoort

Lokeren

Veurne

Torhout

Ghent
(Gent)

Diksmuide

Tielt

Dendermonde

Roeselare

Deinze

Aalst

Ypres
(Ieper)

Courtrai
(Kortrijk)

Oudenaarde

Ninove

Menen

Ronse

Geraardsbergen

Mouscron

Halle

Lessines

Tournai

Ath

Tul

Leuze

Soignies

La Lo

Mons

Ch

Binche

FRANCE

Chim

o less than 10 000 inhabitants
⊙ from 10 000 to 25 000 inhabitants
◉ from 25 000 to 50 000 inhabitants
● from 50 000 to 100 000 inhabitants
⬠ more than 100 000 inhabitants

0   30 M
0   50 KM

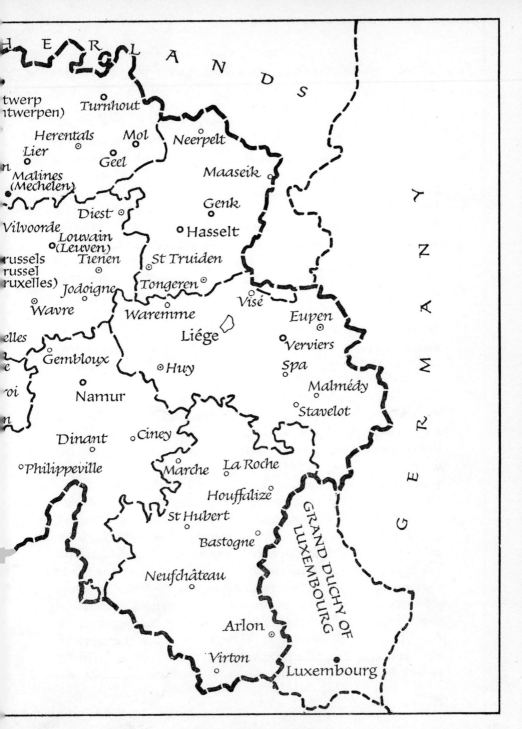

Map of Belgium today

and industry, even industries new and old. It also typifies the Belgian character: vigorous, dynamic, full of earthy common sense – with occasional bursts into public anger.

Belgium today is at the centre of many of the modern world's crucial concerns, especially NATO and the European Communities including the Common Market. It still has a role to play in emerging Africa. The country has always been a crossroads and market-place of Europe. The Belgians themselves have been great internationalists because they are great traders, with one half of their attention on the world and the other fixed on their own domestic quarrels. The contrast of scale seems striking. But the key to Belgium's enigmas lies in the troubled past of this people whose name preceded the Roman Empire, but whose country is still young and still in search of its identity.

Belgium is only a little bigger than Wales or Maryland, one of the smallest but most densely-populated of European countries, with an area of 11,780 square miles for nine and a half million inhabitants. Bounded by the Netherlands in the north, Germany and Luxembourg in the east and France in the south and west, and without natural frontiers except the North Sea coastline, Belgium has been a meeting ground between the Germanic and Latin cultures since Roman times. This has deeply marked Belgium's history by the fact that Flemish, a language of Low German origin almost identical with Dutch, is the traditional speech of the north of the country, while the language of the southern area, roughly equal in size, is French and Walloon dialects closely related to French. This cultural division, established in the northern mists of two thousand years ago, is the cause of most of Belgium's present domestic problems though it has also been a source of great enrichment. There are also some 60,000 German-speaking Belgians around Eupen near the eastern frontier.

However, right at the outset it is important to stress that the country we know as Belgium had no separate existence until the time of the French Revolution. Through many earlier centuries it was considered part of a geographical area that also included the present Netherlands and the Artois of northern France. It was known variously as the Low Countries or Flanders (sixteenth-century Italians spoke of the 'Flemings' of Namur, a town in the heart of Wallonia) and less often Belgica. During this long period the frontier line fluctuated according to the fortunes of the recurrent wars, and the present-day boundaries of Belgium were not fixed until the country emerged as an independent entity in 1830.

Belgium has had the reputation of being a rich country almost throughout its history. But much of the land is not very fertile, nor has it great mineral resources except coal. Its chief natural advantages have always been its rivers, the Meuse and Scheldt and their tributaries, which have made Belgium an easy highway for the commercial traffic of northern Europe. But this accessibility has also cost Belgium dear. The country has been a battleground for innumerable European rivalries. Great Britain has gone to war at least once during each of the last seven centuries – usually to keep the French from controlling the area, because whoever owns it has first-class access to England's south-east coast. France has fought over Belgian territory very much more often, partly to annex the French-speaking areas but also for the strategic advantage of using them as a barrier against the Germans and Dutch. 'The Low Countries would prove an impregnable rampart for Paris,' said Mazarin in 1646, and French strategists agreed with his thinking, both before and after his time.

In physical conformation Belgium falls into three main categories. The coastal district shares the characteristics of the Dutch polder region: behind a line of sand-dunes the land is flat and needs dykes to prevent flooding; it is now well-drained and intensively farmed, but in earlier centuries was a marshy and water-logged plain. Beyond it lies Belgium's low central plateau with agricultural and coalmining areas, and farther south the higher land of the Ardennes rises to over 1,000 feet. This has always been the most thinly populated region of Belgium except in its river valleys. On the uplands a thin chalk soil, heath and forest and a heavy rainfall discourage farming, but the great natural beauty of the area now attracts the hardier tourists.

Belgium also shares the climate of maritime northern Europe. Summers are seldom hot and winters can be cold, especially in the Ardennes; the rainfall averages between 30 and 40 inches a year.

Some five hundred years before the Christian era a number of Celtic or Gaulish tribes moved from the area between the Rhine and the Elbe and settled in the Low Countries. They were defeated by the Romans in campaigns of 57 and 53 BC; Julius Caesar described the Belgae as 'the bravest of all the Gauls'. Once vanquished they adopted the language and the customs of Rome. Tongeren, Namur, Arlon and Tournai became modestly flourishing towns of Belgian Gaul. In the third century, Frankish tribes settled in the northern marshy areas and remained there, neither becoming Romanized nor accepting the Christianity which was then spreading through the Empire.

The Franks also retained their Germanic speech, whereas the Gallo-Romans spoke derivatives of Latin, and the language frontier established at that early date has changed little until the present day. Some historians claim that the ethnic division has also survived, but centuries of contiguity have minimized such differences as there were, and in any case the Belgian Gauls were not of purely Celtic stock.

With the collapse of the Roman Empire in the fifth century, fresh waves of Franks invaded the whole area. By the end of that century a Frankish king, Clovis, left Tournai to conquer for himself an empire stretching from Cologne across northern France, with Paris as its centre. The area was rechristianized when he was baptized into the Roman faith, but Christianity remained a thin overlay above the old pagan religions.

Clovis's weak Merovingian descendants plunged northern Europe into two centuries of strife, which ended only when the mayors of the palace (a family from the Heristal district of the Meuse valley) established themselves as a new dynasty under Pepin the Short. Pepin's great son Charlemagne (758–814) restored stability and a measure of prosperity to Belgium; cloth and metalwork were again produced for sale. Monasteries and bishoprics became centres of Christian learning, as well as providing a rudimentary civil service.

But this peaceful interlude was not to last. In 843 Charlemagne's empire was divided into three parts, with the Low Countries split between France and the Middle Kingdom, Lotharingia; soon the latter was again quarrelled over and subdivided. Into the confusion of civil war came the raids of the Norsemen, who penetrated along the rivers into the heart of the country and repeatedly pillaged.

Throughout the century, until they were finally defeated in a battle at Louvain in 891 by the German emperor, the Normans found that most of the resistance they met came from the great landowners. The wealthiest of these built fortified castles, such as that founded in Ghent by Baldwin Iron-Arm. They established themselves as a military aristocracy owing a nominal duty to the French or German sovereigns, but were effectively independent. By the tenth century the future duchy of Brabant, the counties of Hainaut, Flanders and Namur and the prince-bishopric of Liége already existed in embryo as quarrelsome factions destined to dominate Belgium's history for hundreds of years. The larger townships also began to protect themselves with great walls, and gradually no town of any size was left without them. Slowly, religion reasserted itself; devastated churches were rebuilt; Cluniac abbeys spread; the outline of medieval Belgium began to emerge.

RISE OF THE CLOTH TRADE

Bruges at the end of the gulf of Zwyn became a centre for the wool trade, which had survived from Roman days until the coming of the Northmen. The quality of Flemish textiles caused a demand that exceeded native resources, and by the eleventh century wool had to be imported from England. Its excellence improved the cloth, which soon became unrivalled for flexibility, colour and softness. The demand for it spread from Novgorod to Smyrna as international trade revived. Almost every town in Flanders came to have its weaving industry. Farther to the south, in 'Walloon Flanders', there was a parallel revival of the traditional skills in metalworking. The copper and brass of Dinant, Namur and Huy were widely sold, and contributed to the general rise of prosperity.

Concentration on industrial production led Flanders to need food imports. Grain from across the Rhine, wine and salt from France were bought in exchange for cloth, and the cities of Germany and the Baltic offered dried fish, besides fur, tar, timber and amber. As wealth increased the Belgian towns became eager clients for the

13

pepper, cinnamon, ginger and nutmeg with which medieval Europe spiced its monotonous diet. Later came apricots, figs, raisins and perfumes, damask from Damascus, gauzes from Gaza, muslins from Mosul. Most of these goods were brought by Italian merchants, and the great fairs of Champagne in northern France developed into meeting-grounds for the trade of northern and southern Europe. But when the northern trade grew, Bruges began to replace Champagne as a convenient entrepôt, so that by the thirteenth century Florentines and Venetians, Catalans, Spaniards and Bretons had established permanent depots in Bruges, where they met the agents of the powerful Hanseatic League and the English wool merchants.

TRADE AND TOWNS

The rise of industry and commerce inevitably disturbed the rural social system. Feudalism as it had established itself throughout Europe rested on the peasants, who were tied to their lord's estate as serfs, performing services in return for protection. They produced only as much as the seigneur's household and themselves needed, for self-sufficiency was the accepted rule.

The merchants who established their centres at the junctions of land or water routes had no acknowledged status in the feudal pattern. But by the eleventh century they were already organized into guilds strong enough to negotiate privileges from the local lords. From the first they were acknowledged to be freemen, and their trading posts free 'ports' or communes. The serfs that they attracted to work in them also became free by virtue of their residence. The communes expanded steadily, as we can tell from the growing number of parishes and churches within the town walls – walls which themselves had to be repeated in ever-widening rings. As trade grew there developed an increasing variety of skilled workmen: most important of all were the weavers, shearers, dyers and fullers of the cloth trade, nicknamed the 'blue-nails' because the wool discoloured their hands. Taking into account the help given by wives and children, probably half the total population of Flanders worked in industry by the end of the thirteenth century, an extraordinary circumstance for the Middle Ages.

Most of the towns negotiated charters from the feudal lord of their area. Such charters have acquired somewhat inflated reputations as early models of democracy; in fact they were usually piecemeal documents embodying miscellaneous privileges for the burgher class. But they did, for that class, secure the right to be governed by law and not by the arbitrary wish of a social superior. As their importance increased, the towns also became represented in the provincial parliaments with the clergy and nobles.

Feeding the growing communes led to the large-scale clearing of forests and draining of the Flanders marshes. Despite these land increases the area became one of the most densely populated and highly industrialized parts of Europe. Like present-day Belgium, it was extremely dependent on foreign trade for obtaining the raw materials essential to industry, as well as the food it could not produce in adequate quantities at home. Such dependence made the towns extremely sensitive to foreign wars or to any other disturbance of the lines of communication.

The dependence on external events was felt most keenly by the workers. They naturally understood little of fluctuations in trade, but resented the fact that their wages were low even in times of prosperity. Nor could they easily bring their grievances to any impartial authority; for all power within the cities, both economic and political, lay with the merchants. The charters granted by the overlords gave the merchants the right to make the city laws and to be judges in the law courts. Their class organized the city militia; their taxes built the city walls, as well as houses, schools and churches. And their guilds gradually turned into oligarchies as arrogant as the rural nobility, excluding newcomers and above all the 'common people', who were confined to the crafts and to retail trade. Even without serfdom, a caste system still dominated the communes, in which no worker could hope to rise to high place.

Each trade and craft also had its own guild, not only by the workers' spontaneous wish but because such guilds were easier for the city aldermen to control. Like the merchants' guilds, each one was exclusive in spirit and hostile to competition. However, their protectionism was understandable since their own security was so precarious. Badly housed, poorly paid and cheated with impunity, in periods of trade crisis even skilled craftsmen roamed through the streets or the countryside begging their bread, terrifying the well-to-do by their lawlessness.

BLUE-NAILS AND GOLDEN SPURS

By the mid-thirteenth century strikes began to break out, and for over a hundred years the history of the Low Countries abounds in stories of clashes between the 'good folk', i.e. the ruling class, and the 'blue-nails'. Round the latter gathered the discontented of all crafts. The reaction of the masters to this medieval industrial strife parallels that of nineteenth-century factory owners. They made the city laws harsher. They forbade workers to carry arms or even their tools outside their houses, or to meet in groups. Death became a common punishment for even minor crimes.

In 1280 a virtual revolution broke out when the workers of Bruges, Ypres, Tournai and Douai simultaneously rose, and ran loose through their towns, pillaging, massacring and temporarily taking over the town halls. Terrified, the patricians appealed to the King of France, Philippe le Bel, who helped to restore order at the cost of unleashing ferocious popular hate against French power. From about this time onwards, England began to feature intermittently on the Flemish scene, almost invariably to oppose the extension of French power. In 1302 a weaver, Peter de Coninck, led the men of Bruges in a dawn attack within the city, killing every man who could not correctly pronounce the tricky Flemish phrase *Schild en Vriend* (shield and friend). Virtually every Frenchman in Bruges perished. A few months after this 'Matins of Bruges' a pitched battle followed at Courtrai between the French army and the craft workers who, in a paroxysm of defiant fury, vanquished the French and killed without mercy all who could not speak Flemish. Later this extraordinary fight was called the Battle of the Golden Spurs, from the legend that the field was left strewn with them. Today, each anniversary of the battle is celebrated as a triumph of Flemish patriotism.

During the long period of civil unrest that followed class hatred never subsided, and discontent was intensified by a series of natural

16

catastrophes. Europe suffered some of the worst famines of her history. A series of plagues, including the appalling Black Death, carried off about a third of the population of Europe, as well as causing a steep increase in prices. Other calamities such as the collapse of the great Florentine bankers, and the Hundred Years War between France and England, all had their repercussions on economic life and inevitably inflamed Flanders' social troubles.

In the atmosphere of confusion and strife, workers in different crafts considered all the rest as rivals in the search for wealth; within the cloth trade the 'odious weavers' were everybody's enemies. Consequently the attempts to share city government between patricians, clothworkers and other crafts repeatedly foundered on internal rivalries. Liége, which literally set fire to its rich men in the Mal St Martin, succeeded in maintaining longest the democracy it set up. Ghent's history was especially troubled: time and again, with incredible tenacity, the weavers rose against their masters, while the patricians in turn warred with the Count of Flanders. This constant strife intensified a chronic exodus of weavers, who now emigrated in great numbers to Italy and to East Anglia.

The emigration to England brought a new danger: the English now began to weave their wool at home and to export cloth. The Flemish towns responded to this foreign challenge by competing with each other for wool supplies. Bruges showed a similar blind protectionism when its sea trade suffered as the Zwyn slowly silted up: it tried to compel foreign merchants to remain in the town and to unload their cargoes farther and farther outside it. Commercial and banking activities prolonged Bruges' prosperity, but as a port it was replaced by Antwerp, which offered a fine harbour and greater liberty of trade (for instance, it imported the English cloth that Bruges refused to handle). Only gradually, the cloth merchants and the craft guilds modified their restrictiveness, while the towns began to produce more tapestries, linen, lace and glass. From 1384 the Dukes of Burgundy gradually took the whole of the Low Countries under their control, and helped ease the slow move from a medieval towards a modern economy. Under their rule the fifteenth century became for Flanders a new era of wealth and splendour.

Flanders seems always to have taken particular delight in the colour and show of great occasions, usually connected with the nobility or the Church. But these tastes were never so well gratified as by the House of Burgundy. Duke Philip in particular, who ruled from 1419 to 1467, made his court at Brussels one of the most brilliant in Europe. In 1429 he founded the Order of the Golden Fleece, joining in a characteristic medieval symbol both the Lamb of God and the wool on which his Flemish wealth depended. He used banquets, tournaments and processions as a deliberate policy to win prestige, but they also accorded with his own and his subjects' love of opulent display. He welcomed poets and musicians at his court, and founded the Burgundian library which exists today as one of the treasures of Brussels. Like a Renaissance prince he gave pensions to artists, and himself had the artistic sensibility to appreciate their work.

The Church as well as the ducal court became a great patron of the arts. Saints' days and the great festivals were celebrated with banners and processions: and closely linked with the Church were the great feasts of the guilds, for every occupation had its own saint. There was intense rivalry between the different corporations to see who could put on the best show, just as different towns and different parish churches tried to outdo each other in embellishing their public buildings; this stimulus helped produce an upsurge of artistic genius unmatched anywhere in Europe outside Italy.

Already Flemish architecture had led the way. City walls, fortifications, locks, dykes and bridges had demonstrated the skill of builders and engineers, and soon architects and sculptors showed their artistry was equal to their technical gifts. The example of French Gothic challenged native ingenuity in the construction of cathedrals like those of Ghent, Tournai and Brussels. Some of these were built, added to or improved over several centuries, during which time Flemish Gothic took on its own characteristic and varied forms, illustrated in splendid buildings, many surviving today.

The size and strength of church towers became an object of special pride, so that towers and belfries became features of the town halls, ramparts and churches that dominated the flat plains of Flanders and the riverside cities of the Ardennes. The spire of Brussels' town hall with its brass weather-vane of St Michael remains one of the century's most graceful achievements, as the belfry of Bruges illustrates its solidity and strength. Commercial activity led to the construction of covered market-places such as the famous one of Ypres, and of city halls like those of Louvain and Oudenaarde with their overwhelming profusion of decorative sculpture. Inside, the churches and halls and merchants' houses were equally richly decorated, often with the new tapestries of Brussels and of Tournai which had such a wealth of gold thread mixed into the silk that they were known as cloth of gold; by the brass and copper of Dinant which provided lecterns, baptismal fonts and church plate as well as chandeliers and table-ware for private houses. Sculpture, both in wood and stone, developed a new realism to replace the hieratic figures of saints and the traditional stylized flora and fauna. The carved wooden altarpieces of the Brussels, Antwerp and Malines workshops were exported in great numbers to France, Spain, Germany and even to the Canary Islands. However all this, including the goldsmiths' work, the glass, the illuminations, the printing and engraving (Caxton produced the first printed English book in Bruges in 1475), outstanding as it is, yield pride of place to the genius of the Flemish painters.

The Low Countries had already produced great artists during the fourteenth century, when men had gone out from Brabant and Hainaut and Limbourg to the French court. Their best-known works are probably the exquisite miniatures of the *Très Riches Heures du Duc de Berry* by the Limbourg brothers. Flemish painting indeed probably developed from miniatures, as the extreme delicate exactitude of the work of its leading figure Jan van Eyck seems to indicate. It is no longer believed that van Eyck invented oil painting, but the contemporary admiration for his work helped to spread knowledge of the new technique within the Low Countries and beyond. Van Eyck's gift of realism, coupled with the intense feeling of his religious paintings, were qualities typical of the Flemish genius and were outstanding also in the works of his pupil Petrus Christus, Roger van der Weyden, Hugo van der Goes and many others. The world had seen nothing like the faithful rendering of objects of daily life shown for instance in van Eyck's *Betrothal of the Arnolfini,* or portraits in which the Flemish painters reveal the character of their sitters as well as exact and clear detail of the texture of their garments. The deep spirituality of van Eyck's *Adoration of the Mystic Lamb,* or van der Weyden's Escorial *Deposition from the Cross* impressed even Italian artists and made the influence of Flanders paramount in the religious painting of Germany, Spain, Portugal and Naples as well as attracting to the School of Bruges men like Memling from Mainz, and Dieric Bouts or Hieronymus Bosch now claimed by the Dutch.

As well as their other qualities the paintings of the Flemish school give us a valuable picture of the life of the times. The scarlet turbans and woollen gowns trimmed with squirrel fur, and the elaborately patterned brocades were the characteristic dress of the wealthy classes. The procession of knights towards the Mystic Lamb, on horseback with pennants waving, showed nobles as they might often be seen accompanying their duke. Town and country views were no doubt idealized but there were indeed paved streets, public fountains, houses of brick and stone with glass windows and fireplaces, cleanliness and comfort. By this time the poor were also better off. The kermesses and village weddings of Breughel and Jordaens were painted later, but already we know that the peasants ate and drank their fill at village fêtes, and that they like the town workers crowded the streets and market squares to enjoy the processions, the tableaux vivants and the mystery plays that were spectacular features of the great public occasions.

Flemish literature included a brilliant version of Europe's best-known medieval morality play, *Everyman,* as of the long poem *Reynard the Fox* which later inspired Goethe. The nun Hadewyck wrote verses more heavily charged with mysticism than those of St Teresa of Avila, while an unknown writer from Hainaut composed the enchanting fable of *Aucassin and Nicolette.* Liége in turn gave the world its first adventure story in the *Voyages of Sir John Mandeville,* as Froissart was its first eye-witness reporter describing the splendours of the Burgundian court.

The Chambers of Rhetoric of the fifteenth century began as mere clubs to honour defunct citizens, but developed into literary societies

20

in which each member composed verses as copiously as he drank. They sometimes included poetic jousts with rival communes, featuring the bilingual talents that were common to the people of the southern Low Countries at that time.

Bilingualism is one of the features of this brilliant period. The Burgundian dukes were themselves of French blood and vassals of the French crown, but they encouraged the use of Flemish to emphasize the separateness of the Low Countries from France, a policy that chimed in well with local patriotisms. By 1455 Philip the Good had become overlord of eleven provinces, without counting his domains in France, including Flanders-with-Artois, Brabant, Limbourg, Malines, Antwerp, Namur, Hainaut and Luxembourg.

Never before in the history of the Low Countries had the different marquisates, counties and dukedoms owed allegiance to the same prince. Both economically and politically his reign was a turning-point. He provided the provinces with a uniform and stable gold currency. He made a trade agreement with England, which under different names was renewed well into the next century. By the connexions of his third wife Isabel of Portugal he established Antwerp as the northern terminus for the new Atlantic spice trade. His sailors colonized the Azores. He did a great deal to co-ordinate the different fiscal and legal systems in order to liberate trade; knowing how firmly his peoples were attached to their ancient privileges, he did not touch the traditional regional parliaments, or Estates, but added the new central institution of the Estates-General in which the clergy, nobles and town delegates of the different provinces met together to discuss great questions – usually concerning money. However, the great Flemish cities were notoriously tenacious of their privileges and sooner or later were bound to resist Philip's changes. The worst trouble broke out over his imposition of a salt tax in place of the annual vote of a money grant by the Estates. Ghent went to war with Philip over this, but capitulated when his troops took the city. Two thousand of its citizens were forced to kneel before him in their shirts. He fined them heavily, and took away the city's privilege of controlling the surrounding countryside.

The struggle against the towns intensified under Philip's son Charles the Bold. In 1466, the year before his father's death, Charles razed rebellious Dinant to the ground and threw its inhabitants, tied in pairs, into the Meuse. Two years later he burned and demolished the entire city of Liége brick by brick, slaughtering its inhabitants or drowning them two by two. Even in that brutal age such cruelty excited horror. But Charles died at Nancy in 1477 without achieving his dream of recreating the great Lotharingian Middle Kingdom between France and Germany. Louis XI of France seized on Charles's early death to capture his territories in Burgundy and lay siege to the Low Countries, so that Mary of Burgundy, Charles's only child, was left at nineteen without allies and with nobody to provide money or armies but the communes.

In return for their help they forced Mary to sign the Great Privilege, whereby all the ancient rights of the provinces, towns and guilds were fully restored. This was a natural reaction to Charles's tyranny, but it was a step backwards to medieval parochialism – except that the best charters themselves granted citizens a status long to remain rare in Europe. (Such a charter was the famous Joyous Entry of Brabant, which from 1356 onwards had guaranteed that all citizens of the province were equal before the law, that justice should be open and impartial, that no taxation was valid without consent, and that each man should be free to speak his mother tongue in all his dealings.)

Another stipulation of the Great Privilege was that Mary should marry a husband chosen by the Estates. Their choice fell on Maximilian of Austria, son of the German Emperor Frederick III. Thus the Hapsburgs were brought in to counter French claims; they remained as rulers of the Low Countries for almost three centuries, at the price of endlessly recurring strife with France. Louis XV of France was later to remark with justice, of the tomb of Mary at Bruges: 'There lies the cradle of our wars.'

The reign of the Dukes of Burgundy marked the zenith of Belgium's medieval power and glory, and Belgians have looked back on it ever since as their Golden Age. Perhaps one should say rather as the heart of their Golden Age, because in the longer view the entire

22

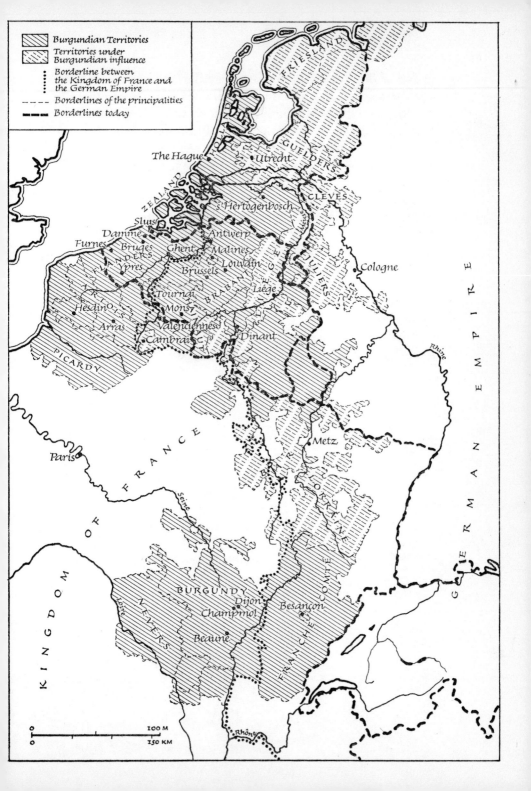

The Hague

Utrecht

FRIESLAND

GUELDERS

HOLLAND

ZEALAND

'sHertogenbosch

CLEVES

Sluis

Damme

Antwerp

JULIERS

Furnes

Bruges

Ghent

Malines

Cologne

FLANDERS

Ypres

Brussels

Louvain

ARTOIS

Tournai

BRABANT

Liége

Hesdin

Mons

Arras

Valenciennes

Dinant

Cambrai

PICARDY

Paris

Metz

LORRAINE

KINGDOM OF FRANCE

Seine

Rhine

GERMAN EMPIRE

BURGUNDY

Dijon

Besançon

Champmol

FRANCHE-COMTÉ

Beaune

NEVERS

Loire

Rhône

100 M

150 KM

period of Belgium's medieval commercial triumphs was also culturally outstanding. Belgium is immensely proud of the fact that their country for a time outshone all the rest of Europe except the Italian cities in painting, in sculpture, music, literature, and in the arts of living, as well as in commercial power. As with the Italian cities, it was a period of war and ruthless cruelty, but it produced the vitality that is the essence of genius.

It was also the time when Belgium was most bilingual – as contemporary Belgians, lost in the present-day language struggle, note with very mixed feelings. But in many other ways the Belgian people are still now what they were then: their flair for industry, their aptitude for commerce, their turbulence and combativeness and their democratic spirit are still very much part of the national character, together with a great love of colour, of pageantry and of roystering good living, including good eating. If ever one can say that there is a crucial period in which a nation crystallizes into being, for Belgium it was their long and glorious Golden Age.

2   Religion and division

THE LINK BETWEEN THE EMPIRE and the Low Countries forced
the latter into a role on the European stage. Previously, political
unrest had been essentially domestic. Foreign affairs had become a
source of strife only because the popular classes tended to want an
alliance between their town and England – which was commercially
important to them but too distant to interfere overmuch – while
the patricians tended to favour the King of France against their
immediate overlords. But from the sixteenth century onward the
area began to be a battlefield on a national and even a continental
scale.

After Mary's accidental death in 1482, Maximilian became regent.
He was opposed to the revival, in the Great Privilege, of the particu-
larism of medieval days, the doctrine that towns, guilds and communes are more important than the state of which they are parts.
Defiantly, Bruges dared to take him captive, and it was then the
cities realized they were now actors on a bigger stage: the German
states sent an army to punish the outrage against their future emperor.
In turn, the arrival of foreign troops to defend a foreign sovereign
provoked the beginnings of a collective resistance. Mary's son
Philip took over the Burgundian inheritance from his father in
1493, and the towns now lost the right to discuss peace and war.
This now became the affair of the Estates-General – the embryo
of the national parliament.

Soon the precarious cohesion of the provinces was stimulated by
common resentment at being a minor concern of their Hapsburg
sovereigns, whose empire became immensely widened when

Philip's wife Joanna of Castile unexpectedly inherited the Spanish dominions of Castile and Aragon, Naples and Sicily, America and the Indies. Philip died while still young; his widow Joanna lost her reason, and their son Charles, born in Ghent in 1500, was therefore destined for all his mother's inheritance as well as the lands of his grandfather Maximilian, now Holy Roman Emperor.

THE NATIVE PRINCE

Charles was brought up in Flanders by his aunt Margaret of Austria, Regent of the Netherlands. Popular because he was a native-born prince who spoke French and Flemish, his people were reluctant to see him leave to claim his Spanish inheritance. After the death of Maximilian in 1519 he was also elected Holy Roman Emperor. In comparison with this vast empire, the Low Countries were a mere drop in his ocean. He went back to them only five times in his forty-year reign, and never for long periods. They became important to him chiefly as sources of revenue, because of his constant wars, particularly against France, whose king, Francis I, worked constantly to weaken Charles's authority in Germany and the Low Countries, as well as exploiting the traditional fealty of Flanders and Artois to the French crown.

Small and unconsidered as they were, the Low Countries felt the repercussions of Charles's problems very deeply throughout his reign. As a Venetian ambassador later remarked, the King's real treasure, his true Indies, lay not in the New World but in the Low Countries.[1] Between 1520 and 1530 alone they gave him no less than 15 million *livres tournois*, over ten million present-day dollars, a fantastic amount for so tiny an area, and this was apart from the vast loans he raised on the money market of Antwerp. So it was politic as well as perhaps sincere for Charles to flatter the land of his birth, saying 'it was the place where his heart remained', surrounding himself for years with Flemish counsellors and above all relaxing for them a little of the harsh fumbling of his centralized administration.

Charles was well served by the Regent Margaret, who ruled till 1530, and later by his sister Mary of Hungary. Under their stewardship the outburst of economic energy already seen under the

Burgundian dukes grew greater yet, stimulated by the geographical discoveries of the age and by the science to which their own great men contributed – notably Mercator, a geographer of Rupelmonde near Antwerp, who invented the cylindrical projection that bears his name.

By this time Antwerp was pre-eminent in Europe for its material prosperity and its cultural life. The inscription borne by its Stock Exchange indicates its internationalism: *Ad usum mercatorum cuiusque gentis ac linguae* (for the use of merchants of whatsoever race or language). Like the rest of the Low Countries it was a centre of good living for 'nothing is done here without eating' said Erasmus. It made itself a centre of the new luxury trades of sugar-refining and diamond-cutting. It inherited the artistic eminence of Bruges, attracting Quentin Metsys, Breughel the Elder, Dürer and Holbein, while Plantin's printing press enhanced the reputation it shared with Louvain as a centre of learning. Antwerp published books of exploration like that of Amerigo Vespucci, and of maps such as Ortelius' first world atlas, while Sir Thomas More even made the gardens of his lodgings at Antwerp the background for his *Utopia*.

No doubt the freedom and welcome given to new ideas caused Antwerp to be one of the earliest homes of Protestantism. Already by 1520 Charles forced the Regent Margaret to institute a state inquisition and to impose the death penalty on heretics. By 1523 the first protestant martyrs, all Lutherans, were burned; but Anabaptism soon became more prevalent until in turn it gave place about 1540 to Calvinism, which became the greatest threat to the *status quo* because its adherents were well organized, literate and disciplined. Charles's edicts against protestantism of any sect became increasingly severe. By 1546 he is estimated to have had at least 50,000 citizens of the Low Countries either buried, strangled, beheaded or burned alive. None the less the provinces continued to react with characteristic traditional stubbornness, and throughout the years the middle classes and artisans remained the backbone of the reform movement.

By 1538 Ghent, unruly as ever, refused to pay more subsidies for wars considered to be entirely in the interests of Spain, and Ghent's example excited the whole of Flanders to revolt. Charles quickly returned, stopped the mob violence, exacted a huge fine, revoked the city's privileges and replaced its democratic government by nominees answerable to him. Then he tightened his control of the entire Netherlands. In 1555, in Brussels, Charles formally handed over the Low Countries and his Spanish kingdom to Philip and himself retired to a Spanish monastery, where he died three years later.

But if Charles had gradually become Spanish-orientated, Philip was foreign to his Netherlands subjects from the start. He knew little of their country and could not speak French fluently, let alone Dutch. Temperamentally also he was alien. He scorned the exuberance of his northern subjects; their rough sports made him literally sick, as did their hearty eating and drinking, while his taste for sombre dress and austere religious devotions contrasted with their love of spectacle. Moreover he was an absent as well as a foreign king. After 1559 he never returned to the Low Countries, though he reigned almost forty years longer.

'STREAMS FATHOMS DEEP' OF WEALTH – AND BLOOD

The financial drain on the Netherlands became acute, but a petition of grievances from the Estates-General, signed by the leading nobles including Prince William of Orange, had little effect. When asked to relax the savage religious policy, Philip renewed his father's severest edict and enforced it with the utmost rigour. Pamphlets condemning everything Spanish – the soldiery, the taxes, Philip himself ('that Spanish swine') – served to fuse political and religious discontent. The methods of the inquisitors and their arbitrary disregard for all Netherlands traditions of justice aroused the resentment even of the predominantly Catholic ruling classes, but Philip refused any changes, and early in the next year two manifestoes, the Compromise of the Nobles and the Confederates' Petition, condemned the inquisition as 'contrary to all laws human and divine'. Rebellious feeling was heightened after a drinking bout in which a group of nobles nicknamed themselves the Beggars, a name that caught on when it was taken to mean general reduction to beggary by Philip.

At the same time a failure of bread supplies caused social misery among the poorer classes that led to a sudden wild outbreak against the churches. Led by Calvinists, it turned into an orgy of iconoclasm. Statues, carvings and pictures in churches all over the land were destroyed in little more than two weeks. Catholic families rallied to the Regent; some hundred thousand refugees escaped for fear of Spanish reprisals and William of Orange retreated to his German estates – wisely as it turned out, for the Duke of Alva, a brilliant general, a fanatical Catholic, a Spanish patriot and no statesman, arrived to root out heresy with pitiless savagery and establish absolutist government. In the next three years he executed at least eight thousand people in violation of every constitutional right. First among them were the Counts Egmont and Horn, though they were neither heretics nor rebels. Their deaths made them a national legend, and to this day they are revered as martyrs in the cause of freedom.

Confiscation of wealth accompanied every death, and did something to fill Spain's permanently gaping coffers. But the 'streams fathoms deep' of wealth that Alva had promised Philip were drying up, so he imposed a perpetual turnover tax of 10 per cent on all commercial transactions. The latter already existed in Spain, then a country 'with an incapacity for economic affairs which seemed almost inspired'.[2] In highly developed Belgium, it led to a universal outcry. Alva in fury reminded the provincial estates that the Holy Office had condemned the entire population to death as heretics, but he suspended the tax for two years in return for a money grant. In turn his unpaid soldiers threw off all discipline, looted, raped and pillaged until Philip himself ordered Alva's recall.

In 1572, when the resistance to the 10 per cent tax was at its height, Dutch privateer ships seized the small town of Brille at the mouth of the Meuse. News of this first success spread like wildfire through the northern provinces so that Holland and Zeeland, Utrecht and Friesland soon declared for the rebel leader, the absent Prince of Orange, who became the great hope of the protestant exiles who had flocked to Holland. Neither Alva nor his successor Requesens could quell the revolt of the northern natives, whose knowledge of the sea and willingness to open the dykes to flood their own lands made them virtually unconquerable. In the end Dutch sea power was to win liberty for the northern Netherlands, as Spanish land power successfully crushed the southern provinces.

But the struggle was not yet over. Mutinous Spanish troops, still unpaid, in November 1575 invaded Antwerp in a frenzy of devastation in which an estimated seven thousand people were killed and the wealth of the city destroyed. The horror of the 'Spanish fury' rallied the Catholics to William despite the nobles' jealousy of his leadership. But when William made a triumphal entry into Brussels late in 1577 the Calvinists' own extremism and their democratic leanings soon threw the Catholic nobles of the south into opposition. With their help the new governor, Don John of Austria, won a victory at Gembloux near Brussels and William was forced to leave.

In July 1584 William was assassinated by a fanatic, and Don John's successor, Alexander Farnese, exploited the confusion that followed by offering terms to the Catholic rebels who still held out.

While the Calvinist Dutch continued to fight, peace of a sort came at last to the southern, or Spanish Netherlands as they were now called. Philip kept them for the Catholic Church and the Spanish crown as he had intended, but it was a pyrrhic victory. His richest provinces had been bathed in blood, many of the most dynamic citizens were killed or exiled, and commerce was totally disrupted.

In return for his subjects' obedience, Philip relaxed his autocratic rule to allow the nobility, the towns and guilds most of their former privileges; but the republican Dutch scorned their Catholic neighbours for acknowledging Philip as their 'natural prince'. The division between the two was further embittered by the contrast between the bustling prosperity of the north and the commercial stagnation in the south. Antwerp's supremacy collapsed, its Stock Exchange became a library, and its international trade passed to Amsterdam. The south enjoyed a sunset glow of artistic splendour in the work of the Breughels, Rubens and Van Dyck, Jordaens and Teniers, but they too were rivalled by Rembrandt and the flourishing Dutch school. In more ways than one the former genius of the Low Countries moved north, so that Holland enjoyed a Golden Century while Belgium was left to endure her Century of Misfortune.

3   People into nation

PHILIP AND HIS CATHOLIC SUBJECTS became reconciled first and foremost because of their common loyalty to the Catholic religion, and secondly because of Philip's preoccupation with other dangers, which made him willing to concede the restoration of the traditional Netherlands rights against arbitrary imprisonment, violation of domicile, confiscation of property or taxation without consent. The people were as deeply attached to these liberties as to the Catholic faith. With both liberty and faith secured, they hoped for a return to the old days, but there were now great material changes, which together seemed to bring about a change of spirit. For the next two centuries turbulent Belgium became a strangely passive country, almost, according to her own historians, a country without a history except of her sufferings as a bloody battleground in other people's wars.

First the Dutch held the Scheldt estuary, which killed the Antwerp trade; secondly, hundreds of thousands of exiled compatriots now became economic rivals in Holland and England; thirdly, Belgium was devastated by repeated invasions. Belgians doggedly repaired their city walls, rebuilt their houses and re-sowed their trampled fields, with a tireless, desperate patience that makes it easy to understand why so many seventeenth-century inns bear the sign *Op Hoop van Vrede* – 'in the hope of peace'.

No doubt their sufferings also added to their new docility, but it is still remarkable that this small corner of Europe, which for so long had been in perpetual ferment, producing out of her turbulence masterpieces of art and of craftsmanship, should now seem to lose her vital force.

Despite the widespread misery the people loved money-making and colourful spectacle as before, and as they still do to this day, and a great many of the public festivities continued as always to centre round the Church. But from now on the robust pleasures were overlaid with an emphasis on suffering, with a brooding mysticism enhanced by Spanish influence. Processions of flagellant penitents who walked barefoot in cassock and cowl were new to the Low Countries, but their deep appeal to the Flemish (if not the Walloon) soul is shown by the survival of such traditions to the present day: the town of Veurne or Furnes near Ostend still has its annual march of barefoot and hooded men, each staggering under the weight of a heavy wooden cross.

During the seventeenth century the clergy was the only section of society that flourished; the Spaniards were openly scornful of all other Belgians. Louvain University had begun a long period of decline, but the religious orders, especially the Jesuits, gained enormous influence. Their convents multiplied everywhere, their baroque architecture and sculpture, their schools and their censorship dominated cultural life. Jansenism, founded by the Bishop of Ypres, had no influence at home. The Bollandist Fathers began their great collection of biographies of saints; but there was virtually no literary output either in French or Flemish. Indeed, Belgium was no longer notable even for riots, although the poor continued to suffer the same degree of misery that had sparked off violent protest in former times.

THE INVADERS

Their plight was worsened by waves of invaders. First were the Dutch, who invaded Flanders in 1600 and from then until their peace with Spain half a century later kept up a never-ending series of frontier raids. When the United Provinces achieved their full independence in 1648, Belgium in turn became the prize that Louis XIV coveted in his search for France's 'natural' frontiers. The struggle between French Bourbon and Spanish Hapsburg continued intermittently from Louis's first attack in 1667 until 1713, in a series of shifting alliances that involved much of European territory and always the Spanish Netherlands.

England was concerned as always that the territory should not fall under French domination, and became alarmed when Louis won Douai, Tournai, Oudenaarde, Lille and Courtrai in easy conquests that were spectacles to which he invited his mistresses. Encouraged by these successes, Louis decided also to overthrow the Dutch Republic, whose citizens he scorned as 'cheese merchants and maggots'. The union of the Dutch and English crowns under William III in 1689 strengthened the two countries' resistance, although Louis's generals sacked Brussels in 1695, reducing the famous Grand'Place to a mass of smoking ruins.

The Peace of Ryswick gave a breathing space, but war soon broke out again over French claims to the Spanish throne. A new coalition under the generalship of the Duke of Marlborough inflicted Louis's first severe defeat at Blenheim, and followed this up by resounding victories on Belgian soil at Ramillies, Oudenaarde and Malplaquet. As a result, the Treaties of Utrecht and Rastadt of 1713 and 1714 put an end to Spanish possession of the Netherlands, which were now given to the Austrian Hapsburg Charles VI as part of the European package deal.

Belgian opinion, of course, was not consulted. The Treaty of Utrecht also adjusted the frontiers with France, confirming Louis's possession of Valenciennes, Cambrai, Lille, St Omer and Dunkirk, now lost to Belgium for ever. By a series of Barrier Treaties Holland also won the right to station Protestant troops in fortresses on Belgian soil, at the expense of the local inhabitants. 'The Barrier Treaties,' comments a Belgian historian, 'mark the moment of our lowest political, economic and social humiliation.'[1]

AUSTRIAN RULE
However, Charles VI promised to respect the traditional rights of his new subjects, despite the growing prevalence of absolutist rule in Europe. He never visited his new territories but ruled through deputies who continued the Spanish type of government, somewhat more efficiently. In an attempt to encourage trade with the East Indies the Austrian government created the Ostend Company, but the jealousy of England, Holland and France led them to suppress it

in 1723, and the country was left with no outlets but its own domestic markets. This led to increased dyking, draining and cutting of canals and the development of farm methods much admired by English agriculturalists. The rich soil of the Flemish polders gave new crops of tobacco, beetroot, turnips and clover. Potatoes began to replace bread in the diet of the poorer classes. Hops provided beer for the national drink, and flax and hemp stimulated the textile industry, which took on a new importance with the invention of the flying shuttle. The manufacture of woollens developed in the Verviers region, near Liége, in fact, was now continuing a long and steady rise to affluence. Being independent of Spain, the principality had largely escaped the religious wars and the tradition of democratic opposition to the prince-bishop encouraged anti-clerical sympathies, so that protestants were welcomed and industries profited accordingly. Production of iron grew as coal replaced charcoal for smelting; there was a brisk sale for firearms as well as for sheet iron, hardware and coal. Best of all, Liége had an outlet through the Meuse to the Rhine estuary, so that her goods could be exported.

For many years the Austrian Netherlands were blessedly free from invasion, except during the War of the Austrian Succession when they were occupied for three years by French troops. Restored in 1748, they were ruled by the Empress Maria Theresa's brother-in-law Charles of Lorraine for the next thirty-six years. Under this easy-going prince the country enjoyed a certain bucolic prosperity. Only about three per cent of the population was literate, and the people resisted Maria Theresa's attempts to foster state secondary schools. Intellectual life stirred again when the writings of the French philosophers reached Belgium despite the strict ecclesiastical censorship; but Voltaire's description of the life of Brussels reflects that of the country in general at this time:

> Pour la triste ville où je suis
> C'est le séjour de l'ignorance
> De la pesanteur, de l'ennui,
> De la stupide indifférence.
> Un vieux pays d'obédience
> Privé d'esprit, rempli de foi.

('As for this dreary city, it is the home of ignorance, of dullness and boredom, of stupid indifference. An aged country of obedience, empty of wit and filled with faith.')

Joseph II's visit after he became Emperor in 1780 at first delighted his subjects, who had received no sovereign on their soil since 1659, but the impatience of this enlightened despot with the 'antediluvian rubbish' of local privileges soon antagonized everybody. However, the first target of his reforming zeal was the Church. The convents of the contemplative orders were suppressed. Public office was opened to non-Catholics; parish registers of births, marriages and deaths were taken out of the hands of the clergy and entrusted to state officials. Almost worse was a decree concerning the *kermesses* and *ducasses*, that is the religious festivals including costumed processions, which usually involved much eating and drinking and often ended in drunken brawls. All such celebrations were to take place on the same day throughout the country. When Joseph also made a clean sweep of the traditional administrative and judicial systems, he had offended the entire population – clergy, nobles, lawyers, merchants and the pious poor. Their hostility was not lessened even by Joseph's success in evacuating Dutch troops from the Barrier forts.

THE CONSERVATIVE REPUBLIC

As so often in Belgium's history, opposition did not lead to unanimous action; from 1787 onwards two factions emerged. The first, led by a Brussels lawyer, Henri Van der Noot, and supported by the aristocracy, the clergy, leaders of the corporations and the peasants, demanded a complete return to the old ways. A much smaller number of clergy and nobility, together with army officers and lawyers, favoured some reform but deplored Joseph's drastic methods and his centralization of all authority in Vienna. These 'progressives' grouped round a Flemish advocate, François Vonck, and at first helped Van der Noot create a Patriotic Committee, whose colours were the black, yellow and red of the present-day Belgian flag (black for the province of Brabant, yellow for Flanders and red for Hainaut).

Together they formed a volunteer regiment which in 1789 took Ghent and Bruges, and wrung some concessions out of Joseph. Excited by the revolution in France, they proclaimed Joseph's deposition, and in January 1790 Van der Noot's faction, breaking with the Vonckists, set up the Republic of the United States of Belgium. The constitution of this short-lived republic included sentences translated word for word from the United States of America's Declaration of Independence; but most of it harked back to the sixteenth century and was no more, according to its Vonckist critics, than an 'aristo-theocratic cabal'. The clergy then accused the Vonckists of being enemies of religion; peasants invaded Brussels and pillaged the houses of their sympathizers, who fled into exile in France.

Soon after Joseph's death in February 1790 the republic was overthrown by a small Austrian army. Leopold II restored government as practised under Maria Theresa, and for the next few months Liége became a new focus of disturbance. The principality did not form part of the Austrian Netherlands. Linked by language and by sympathies with revolutionary France, Liége acclaimed the fall of the Bastille with wild enthusiasm, took its town hall by storm, forced the prince-bishop into exile and proclaimed universal suffrage. But Austrian troops soon brought back the government, and the revolutionaries were exiled. Together with Vonckists they formed in Paris the *Comité des Belges et Liègeois Unis*, and urged the French to help them liberate Belgium. In 1792 France declared war on the Austrian Emperor, and occupied the whole of Belgium once more. Repulsed by the Austrians, they returned again after their victory at Fleurus in 1794, and this time stayed for twenty years.

ANNEXATION TO FRANCE

At first welcomed as friends everywhere except in Flemish Brabant and Flanders, the French soon became widely unpopular. Making an even cleaner sweep than Joseph II, they denounced the privileges of clergy and nobility. In the name of the equality of citizens before the law they suppressed all Belgium's venerable charters, divided the country into nine provinces, and set up an administrative and judicial system very similar to that of Joseph II. Like him, they made education and the keeping of parish registers the affair of the state. Although many of these reforms appear in the present constitution of Belgium, at the time they profoundly shocked conservative opinion, as did the increasing anti-clericalism of the French Convention and Directoire. In 1797 Austria – to England's dismay – formally ceded her Belgian provinces to France, but Belgian hopes of better treatment did not materialize. On the contrary, heavy taxation, compulsory military service and constant affronts to the Church caused widespread sullen hostility. Under Napoleon the restoration of Catholicism as the state religion brought some appeasement of discontents, though the Empire was never popular. The country passively accepted Napoleon's centralizing reforms, the civil code, the new coinage and the change of weights and measures, and of taxation: even government control of secondary education, the submission of the clergy to the state and the non-return of confiscated Church lands caused little outcry. The wealthy classes, who had the capital to buy Church property, profited from the Revolution in this and other ways. With the Scheldt at last opened, and all France as a market, the nascent industries of Belgium enjoyed a minor boom – no longer impeded by the rigidity of guilds and corporations. Metal-working, wool-spinning and weaving and coal production increased; and the first cotton-spinning machinery on the Continent was set up when Lieven Bauwens of Ghent smuggled from England the secret of the spinning jenny.

After Napoleon broke with the Pope in 1811, French rule began to be openly resisted. The clergy encouraged young men to hide in the woods and forests to escape conscription; and as Napoleon's government became in effect a police régime, with arbitrary arrests and ever-increasing exactions, public hostility grew until by the time of Waterloo only Liége remained loyal to France. Hatred of France was strongest in the Flemish provinces, where use of the Flemish language was banned for all official purposes. There was no popular uprising as the Empire broke up, but some Belgian troops fought alongside the Allies in the battles of Quatre-Bras and Waterloo.

At the Congress of Vienna Britain's desire for a solid bulwark against France led Lord Castlereagh to propose a union of the ex-Austrian Netherlands with the Dutch United Provinces under the sovereignty of William of Orange. This seemed a reasonable arrangement, as the two parts of the Low Countries at least made a viable economic unit. Indeed, access to Dutch world-wide shipping more than compensated Belgium for the loss of her French markets, and offered a severe potential challenge to England's own export trade. This was an economic price that Britain was willing to pay for her strategic advantage; none the less, neither Holland nor Belgium was enthusiastic for the proposed union. Belgians wished to return to Austrian rule, which increased traditional Dutch scorn for their apparently subservient neighbours; while Belgians shrank from alliance with Calvinism. However, the four Allies (England, Prussia, Austria and Russia) decreed the creation of the new Kingdom of the Netherlands, excluding Luxembourg province but including the principality of Liége. William swore to govern under a constitution giving civil and religious liberty to all his subjects; and for a while it seemed the shotgun marriage might turn out well.

William did a great deal to foster Belgian industry. He had new roads built, and a great new canal dug to join Ghent to the North Sea. Antwerp again became a thriving port. An enormous increase in coal production resulted from the introduction of the Newcomen steam pumps and the Davy lamp. John Cockerill of Haslington in Lancashire founded one of Belgium's greatest industrial enterprises around Seraing near Liége. With some royal help, Cockerill developed ironworks, blast furnaces, rolling mills, forges, mining machinery and glassworks on a scale then unknown in continental Europe. The textile industries also prospered. In 1822 William founded the *Société Générale*, an industrial bank destined to become a world-wide financial power.

But William's authoritarian ways antagonized his Belgian subjects. He taxed them unfairly by dividing the public debt in two, though Holland's had been twelve times greater than that of Belgium. Seats in the parliament were also shared equally although the

Belgian population outnumbered the Dutch by over a million; and there was an unfair proportion of Dutchmen in the administration. William claimed that this Dutch predominance was justified by Belgium's far higher proportion of illiterates and consequent scarcity of men suitable for office. He set up a state system of education from primary to university level, including state universities at Ghent and Liége; but this was inevitably opposed by the clergy, who from the beginning had felt 'consternation in their souls' about Calvinist William's rule. Even his decree that the Dutch language should be taught and officially used in the Flemish provinces failed to please Catholic Flanders. Matters grew worse when he also tried to control the training of young priests.

Until then, a large part of the prosperous bourgeoisie, influenced by the values of the French Revolution, had approved William's anti-clerical measures; but he antagonized them also by his increasing severity against the Press and against freedom of speech. In 1828 the Catholic and Liberal parliamentary parties joined together, with the Church's support, to petition William for greater liberty – especially freedom to associate and to control education. The unexpected union of Liberals and Catholics disconcerted William. Encouraged, they presented a second monster petition demanding a limitation of the King's powers by giving real authority to parliament. William played for time, and passions mounted until, in July 1830, Belgium's French neighbours once more set an example by throwing out their own autocratic sovereign in the name of liberty.

THE REVOLUTION

Ever since 1815 Bonapartists in France had looked for an opportunity to wipe out the humiliation of Waterloo; other Frenchmen still cherished expansionist policies. In 1829 the Prime Minister, Prince Polignac, drew up a plan to seize Belgium by force. French agents were active in fomenting Belgian discontents, and some of the young Belgian zealots began to talk of union with France, in place of the administrative separation of Belgium from Holland under the Dutch crown, which by now the union of the Catholics and Liberals was demanding. A prominent Liberal, Alexandre Gendebien, urged full partnership with France in an article which was distributed at the entrance to the Monnaie Theatre on the evening of 25 August 1830, before the performance of an opera, *La Muette de Portici*, which had had immense impact when first performed in Paris two years before. Its plot concerned a seventeenth-century Neapolitan revolt against Spanish rule. With each song of revolution the audience became wildly excited; and in the fourth act, the tenor's impassioned

> *Amour sacré de la patrie*
> *Rends-nous l'audace et la fierté*[2]

brought almost every man in the house to his feet and into the street.

Rioting and plundering began and continued for several days. The young bourgeois rebels could never have won, however, if there had not been a simultaneous outbreak of machine-smashing among Belgium's unemployed and ill-paid workers, who had suffered greatly during the swift upsurge of industrial development. The black, yellow and red flag of the 1790 republic reappeared. The mob began to shout *Vive la Belgique* and the volunteers of the national guard sang the new anthem, the *Brabançonne*, written for them by the Frenchman Jenneval. On 20 September the Brussels crowd attacked the town hall: William's son Frederick marched on the capital, and was met by barricades in the Royal Park, manned by young bourgeois, by workers and peasants, and by volunteers from Liége, Louvain and France. They held out for days, until Frederick withdrew his troops. The fighting cost the rebels 1,800 dead, but soon gave them control of the entire country except Antwerp. A provisional government proclaimed the independence of the Belgian provinces, and the country quickly elected a National Congress charged with drawing up a constitution.

In the meantime William appealed to the Allies of 1815, who had watched developments in Brussels with surprise and alarm; but Lord Palmerston, the new British Foreign Minister, was sympathetic to the Belgian independence movement though the other Allies, Austria, Russia and Prussia, were not. But nobody wanted war, and on 20 December the four Allies, together with France, acknowledged Belgium's independence at a conference in London and bound

40

themselves to guarantee her perpetual neutrality, within frontiers that excluded Limbourg and Luxembourg. They considered this handsome treatment; but the new country was not grateful. Exhilarated and inexperienced, delegates to the Brussels Congress rejected the proposed frontiers, repudiated the guarantee of neutrality as a limitation on their freedom to make alliances, and promptly voted to offer the crown to the Duke of Nemours, young son of Louis Philippe. They did this, they said, because France alone had sympathized with their aspirations; and with the irreverence of David defying Goliath, the Congress threatened war if the London Conference did not meet all its demands.

Louis Philippe was flattered and embarrassed by Belgian gratitude. But in London his minister Talleyrand cynically suggested that in view of Belgian defiance their country should be dismembered, France taking the French-speaking provinces and Prussia those beyond the Meuse. William could be given the Flemish-speaking areas and Great Britain could make a second Gibraltar of the Meuse and Scheldt estuaries. All but England believed this would serve the Belgians right; but Palmerston's refusal to give France anything at all barred the way to partition, and earned him some sort of right to his title of 'the father of Belgium'. Following Palmerston's lead, all the Great Powers promised Belgium some satisfaction over frontier questions, but insisted on her neutrality. In Brussels a leading deputy, Joseph Lebeau, faced an angry and excited Congress and denounced the political *naïveté* of favouring France when it was clear that England would not tolerate Belgium's becoming a French protectorate. But the Congress still preferred Nemours, and was crestfallen when Louis Philippe refused the throne on his son's behalf. Meanwhile, several of the most prosperous cities, including Ghent and Antwerp, came out in favour of a continuing link with Holland. The clash between Orangist supporters and the 'French' party seemed ready to plunge the young state into anarchy. A native nobleman was chosen as Regent but was totally ineffective; and as the crisis grew, Lebeau proposed a new candidate, Prince Leopold of Saxe-Coburg-Gotha.

This forty-year-old German aristocrat belonged to the class of

Europe's ruling dynastic families. As a young man he had served in the Russian army against Napoleon: in 1816 he became a British subject when he married the heiress to the English throne, Princess Charlotte. He remained in England after her tragically early death the following year and only returned to European prominence when in 1830 he was offered, but refused, the throne of Greece. A Belgian delegate in London, Sylvain Van der Weyer, had proposed Leopold's name as king in November 1830 but it was Lord Palmerston who again influenced the final decision. Leopold was English by culture and sympathy; better still, he was a widower and could marry one of Louis Philippe's daughters, which would be a neat way of satisfying the pro-French sympathies of many Belgians. True, he was a Protestant; but he was believed to be wise and fair-minded, perhaps the very man to hold the balance between Belgium's Catholics and anti-clericals if their alliance should not last. Besides, any children of his future marriage would, as native-born Belgians, be brought up in the Catholic faith. On 4 June the Congress elected him king by 152 votes out of 195.

But prudent Leopold would not lead this rash people unless it made its peace with the powers of the London Conference. After a little more haggling the Allies agreed to a settlement embodied in eighteen Articles which became the birth certificate of the new nation, and Leopold accepted the crown without further delay, though it horrified much of European royalty. To them, the Belgian people were headstrong revolutionaries; the Austrian Emperor Francis II commented: 'I'm sorry for the man, because I know that people. Nobody will ever be able to satisfy them.' But Leopold's good looks and his dignity won him an enthusiastic reception everywhere; his journey through Belgium became more and more a Joyous Entry, culminating in the welcome he received from Brussels on 21 July.

That day marked for him, as for his country, a new beginning. In the Place Royale, from which the barricades were now removed, the revolutionaries' young tree of liberty shivered in the breeze, opposite the gilded throne that stood empty on the topmost step of St Jacques' church. Near it the banners of the provinces recalled Belgium's proud glories; the new black, yellow and red flag waved everywhere. Before Leopold and the assembled Congress, the Regent formally relinquished his powers, the oddly-named Vilain Quatorze read the new Constitution, and Leopold swore to respect it as the embodiment of the liberties of the Belgian people. So, without a coronation and without holy oil, on the steps of a church but not inside it, the Belgians, a new nation but an old people, chose for their royal republic a king who knew little of them and bore no drop of their blood in his veins. Among cries of *Vive le Roi*, the president of the Congress, Count de Gerlache, solemnly gestured Leopold to the lonely eminence that awaited him, saying: 'Sire, mount your throne.'

4　The kingdom means business

BELGIUM'S BIRTHPANGS did not, alas, end with Leopold's accession. Only a few days later William of Holland suddenly invaded, swearing 'that man has robbed me before of my wife, and now of my kingdom'.[1] The Belgian army, ill-equipped and undisciplined, fell away before the Dutch attack; and Leopold appealed for British and French help. Louis Philippe immediately sent in 50,000 men. At Louvain they turned back William's troops without a battle, and lingered in Belgium until Palmerston bluntly warned France that their continued presence would mean war. But they had saved Belgium's independence.

After this inglorious ten-day campaign the Belgians were obliged to accept a less favourable new Treaty of 24 Articles, by which they were to forfeit half of each of the two provinces of Limbourg and Luxembourg; but in fact Belgium held on to them because William refused to recognize the treaty. For seven years longer he menaced the new state, despite joint British and French action that deterred any new attack; one of Leopold's tasks was therefore to reorganize the army, which he did with some help from Napoleon's nephew Murat, who lived in Brussels with his wife, George Washington's great-niece. Another enterprise was to arrange his wedding with Louis Philippe's eldest daughter, Louise-Marie. A girl of twenty, Louise accepted the match without enthusiasm and turned out to be a good wife but an indifferent queen. Her shyness made her seem expressionless in public, whereas a little warmth might have charmed her exuberant subjects and offset Leopold's own natural coldness. However, the marriage pleased the country, especially since three sons were born of it and the future of the dynasty was thereby secured.

The major enterprise for King and parliament during these early years was the smooth running-in of the brand-new engine of state – the constitution voted by the National Congress in February 1831. This was admired throughout the nineteenth century as a model of liberal ideals; and it is indeed a remarkable achievement, given the troubled circumstances in which it was conceived. With Dutch William's autocratic methods fresh in their memories, its drafters had intentionally placed power in the hands of ministers responsible to parliament and not to the King. Leopold had commented when he first saw it, 'you have been rough on royalty'. But the reverse side of Belgians' suspicion of monarchical abuses was their sincere faith in liberty. This faith was shared equally at that time by Liberals and Catholics, the latter influenced by the Catholic reformer Lamennais, the Liberals by the two French Revolutions, and both parties by memories of the best in Belgium's own long traditions.

The constitution guaranteed the historic liberties, including freedom from arbitrary arrest or punishment, the right to be tried in public and to own property, and the inviolability of the home, together with freedom to petition, to bring action against public administrators, to pay only agreed taxes, and freedom of choice of language. Modern additions were freedom of speech, of the Press, of assembly and association, of education and of religious worship. Church and state were to be separate, but in recognition of the social utility of religion and of the loss of Church endowments, the state allotted grants to all denominations for the stipend of pastors and the maintenance of places of worship.

The King had the power to appoint ministers, even from outside parliament, but his choice had to have parliamentary approval. No law could receive the royal assent until parliament passed it. The King had the right to veto any measure, but could not take action himself unless it was countersigned by at least one minister. In no case could an order from the King remove responsibility from a minister. Under certain circumstances the King had the right to dissolve parliament. He commanded land and sea forces, and had the right to declare war and to make treaties of peace, of alliance and of commerce, making public as much information on these as the interest and security of the state allowed.

The parliament was to consist of two Chambers, of Representatives and of the Senate, with equal powers except for some priority for the lower House on budgetary questions. Only men with stringent property qualifications had the right to vote.

The country was divided into nine provinces, with names recalling the medieval principalities. Each province was to be ruled by a governor appointed by the King, with an elected provincial council of limited powers; but the communes were given the wide autonomy inherited from the Middle Ages, with virtually independent local government.

From the start, Leopold made the fullest use of all the constitution allowed him. By appointing and dismissing ministers, indefinitely delaying his signature to bills he disliked, and dissolving the Chambers when he thought fit, he gradually came to possess more effective power than the drafters of the constitution had envisaged. Through his position as commander-in-chief of land and sea forces he became his own Minister for War; and his close relationship to half the ruling houses of Europe made him virtually Foreign Minister also. Although this situation has evolved since Leopold's day, he set a precedent of effective royal authority which itself has become a tradition, so that right up to the present time the Belgian king plays a greater role in his country's affairs than other remaining European sovereigns.

CATHOLIC-LIBERAL UNION

In one important case, however, his attempt to influence foreign affairs failed. When William unexpectedly agreed to sign the 24 Articles in 1838, Leopold tried to arrange through his niece Victoria for Belgium to keep the whole of Luxembourg and Limbourg. But England like the rest of the Powers wanted to finish the entire affair. The Belgians were angered once more by the prospect of losing territories that had been theirs since the fifteenth century; but they were obliged to accept the Treaty, which was signed at last on 19 April 1839, together with the five-power guarantee of neutrality, which remained in force until Germany tore it up as a 'scrap of paper' in 1914. 'This country feels humbled and disenchanted with its so-called political independence,' Leopold told Victoria; and he stressed that Belgian anger was principally directed against England.[2] This was a little unjust, since all the Powers had been equally adamant about the two provinces; but it helped to develop a love-hate relationship with England that survives as a living tradition in Belgium right to the present day.

The separation from Holland again faced Belgium with the problem of finding markets for her goods. To replace the lost Scheldt waterway, John Cockerill suggested a railroad network using the newfangled English steam-engines. Ministers Lebeau and Rogier carried out this daring and visionary scheme as a State enterprise; and the first continental European railroad was inaugurated on 5 May 1835 in the presence of George Stephenson, with a triumphant run from Brussels to Malines (and a less glorious return – the train in which King Leopold travelled got over-excited and stopped dead). Within a decade, business confidence had revived, banks and credits multiplied, and industries developed so fast that Belgium was the only European country to keep abreast of the world's pace-setter, England. English engineers, English artisans and English patents were found everywhere, so that in these early years Belgium was industrially as closely linked to Britain as in political sympathies she was to France. Throughout this time, Belgian workers remained victims of sudden unemployment or of price rises, but nobody thought the state should intervene. A government inquiry begun in 1846 revealed appalling poverty and malnutrition; but little was done, and the poor were too passive to complain.

Once the threat from Holland was over, and Belgium's industry began to find its feet, the government coalition began to dissolve. Catholics and Liberals could not agree on the right relations between Church and State; Catholics believed the State should be enclosed within the Church, while the Liberals insisted on exactly the reverse; and both aimed to control education so as to propagate their own views. Like Leopold I, the Belgian clergy had made the fullest use of all the rights the constitution gave them. Churches grew numerous and wealthy once more; seminaries and religious orders multiplied. Louvain University re-established itself as a Catholic foundation in 1834, and in return the Freemasons founded the University of Brussels; the two were destined to long and bitter rivalry. At their first big congress in 1846, Liberals expressed their concern at the 'strangehold' of Catholicism over education in rural districts. They demanded that all grades of instruction should be supervised by the State, and put their resolutions into effect during the middle years of the century, in which they held almost continuous power under two doctrinaire leaders, Charles Rogier, a hero of the revolution, and a gifted Liége lawyer, Frère-Orban.

LIBERAL GOVERNMENT

One of the first tasks for the Liberals was to keep Belgium calm and safe during the wave of revolutions that shook many European states during 1848; but despite a run on the banks there was surprisingly little political excitement. The cabinets resisted Leopold's urgent advice to spend more money on national defence, and were soon concentrating on the purely domestic threat of the Catholics' near-monopoly of education.

In 1850 Frère-Orban decreed that sixty secondary schools should be built, under state control. The bishops promptly put the new schools under interdict, and in return Belgian freemasonry came to the fore as the champion of state education, free of clerical influence. Relations between the two worsened again when a Catholic ministry passed a 'law of the convents' in 1857, reversing an act that gave the state control of charitable donations. A sudden series of anti-clerical riots alarmed everybody; but worse was to follow. As the doctrinaire Liberals became more aggressively anti-Catholic, the Catholic clergy called on their flocks to resist, so that for the first time in independent Belgium the masses became involved in political quarrels.

For a time, a new focus for dispute was the city of Antwerp. Leopold was trying hard to push through parliament the plans of a military engineer, Brialmont, to make Antwerp a giant fortress in which practically the entire population could shelter in time of war.

The city believed this fortress would ruin its thriving commerce; Liberal opinion was hesitant, especially about the expense; but the Church was determinedly anti-military and made an all-out attack on the government, using the new technique of giant rallies which became known as *meetinguisme*. Against it the Liberals put up an incoherent resistance, divided as they were between those who scorned the lower classes, and the progressives who wished like the Catholics to appeal to them, and were willing to outbid the Church by offering universal suffrage and elementary education for everyone. Meanwhile, as internal dissension mounted, the country's prosperity grew, stimulated by the re-opening of the Scheldt in 1863 after Belgium bought up the Dutch tolls, and by the triumph of the free-traders against traditional protectionism. Thus the face of Belgium was greatly changing when Leopold I died in December 1865.

Leopold had been revered by his people, if not warmly loved, and his personal prestige in Europe had been useful to his country. His son Leopold II did not inherit this European eminence; but he was Belgian born, a Catholic, and soon led his compatriots in their passion for industrial and scientific progress. Even before his accession he had drawn up plans for developing Belgium's chief towns, in his abiding wish to make his country a showplace for urbanism as well as for industry.

However, he and his fellow-countrymen were soon to learn that their very independence still remained precarious. In 1870, on the eve of the Franco-Prussian war, the German chancellor Bismarck revealed a secret document in which Napoleon III had proposed that France should annexe Belgium, and Germany, Holland. Outraged, Gladstone forced both countries to renew their 1839 guarantees of Belgian neutrality; and England held 20,000 men ready to fight if Belgium were invaded during the war that followed. After Germany's victory the mortified French abandoned their centuries-old aim of conquering Belgium, and dreamed instead of recovering Alsace and Lorraine. In Belgium, the anti-militarist majority rejoiced that their homeland had come unscathed through the peril of European war, and left Leopold to press unsuccessfully for many years for men and money. Another period of tension between

France and Germany in the 1880s led parliament reluctantly to consent to fortify the Meuse valley between Liége and Namur;[3] otherwise Belgians continued to pin their faith on the international guarantees of their neutrality and to concentrate their full attention on domestic affairs.

THE SCHOOL WAR

None the less, outside influences helped the development in Belgium, as elsewhere, of dangerously different ideologies. The positivist teachings of Auguste Comte and the discoveries of Charles Darwin led many young Liberals to make a religion of science and to become impatient with Catholic 'shibboleths'. They believed that the instructed intelligence could solve all mysteries, and this heightened their determination to take education out of the hands of the Church.

At the same time, the latter increased its mystical defence against the intrusions of science: new cults such as that of the Sacred Heart had very wide success. After 1870, when Rome lost its temporal power, its spiritual appeal grew stronger. The danger point for Belgium came when many of the faithful, knowing Pius IX's dislike of liberalism, began to turn against their own liberal constitution as a gesture of loyalty to the Holy See. The Papal nunciate in Brussels became a centre for Catholic malcontents;[4] and the Liberals were quick to denounce and exaggerate this treachery to the State. 'From papal vermin deliver our country' became a favourite Liberal song picked up by the Brussels crowds; while popular Catholic papers described liberalism as 'invective, lies, insults, spit, slaver and mud'. In every commune there were rival Liberal and Catholic butchers, grocers and every other kind of enterprise, as well as a spoils system for municipal employees. Liberals wore cornflowers in their buttonholes and attacked religious processions with their walking sticks, while Catholics wore poppies and desecrated Liberal funerals. Groups with pink banners clashed with blue-bannered groups in the streets, while Flemish nationalists began to brandish green banners against everybody who spoke French, greatly adding to the heated confusion.

50

In 1878 the doctrinaire Liberal Frère-Orban was back in power, and within a few months had prepared a new law on education, one of whose main aims was to correct the 1842 law on primary schools. This had decreed that each commune should provide an elementary school, either Catholic or not, according to local preferences. In rural districts the communes had almost invariably favoured Church schools, while most big towns had built lay schools and had dropped the compulsory religious teaching. The new law said that all communes were now to provide a non-Church school under the control of the State, staffed by teachers with state diplomas. Religious instruction was to be optional, and given outside school hours. For older children there was to be a carefully organized choice of studies to fit them for future occupations. Many of the provisions for advanced education were excellent, but there was no possible chance of the law's being adopted. Apart from offending the deep faith of the majority of Belgians, it flew in the face of communal independence, and of the constitutional principle of educational freedom. This 'law of disaster' unleashed an unprecedented public storm, led by the clergy who threatened the faithful with excommunication for any contact with the godless new schools. Money rapidly poured in to build and endow rival Church foundations, so that 65 per cent of all children attending school had moved into them in less than two years. In return, the government stopped the pay of troublesome priests, though the Liberals were alarmed by the storm they had raised and even more troubled when the Church boycotted the celebrations of fifty years of national independence, thus appearing once more to withdraw Catholic loyalty from the Belgian State. Only a few years later, however, in 1884, the Catholics inflicted a crushing electoral defeat on the Liberals and were to exercise parliamentary control continuously until the outbreak of World War I.

Eager to repair the damage, the Catholics passed two new school laws in quick succession. Religious instruction was made compulsory in all schools. Otherwise, control was handed back to the communes, who could either maintain a lay school or 'adopt' a Catholic one; only the schools of their choice would be entitled to state subsidies.

But the suppression of the Ministry of Education, and a relaxation of state control of teachers' training colleges, meant that teaching again became unco-ordinated and piecemeal, and except in wealthy communes standards often fell. By 1910 10 per cent of the total population was estimated to be illiterate, the highest proportion being found in rural Flanders. Another evident result was that non-Catholic schools in Catholic communes risked total lack of support, and could sometimes only pay their teachers starvation salaries. Within a short time, fourteen of the country's communes protested against this in a petition to Leopold which they called the Compromise of the Communes, in imitation of the Compromise of the Nobles of 1566. Leopold could not alter the law of the land, but he did secure the services of a moderate Catholic minister, August Beernaert, who kept the Catholic extremists in check. Beernaert also helped Leopold face trouble that now loomed ahead from two other sources: one was the King's Congo venture, described in Chapter 8, and the other was the rise of the socialist movement.

WORKERS AND SOCIALISM
By the 1880s heavy industry had spread along the valleys of the Meuse and the Sambre, around Mons and Charleroi, Liége and La Louvière, where coal mines, steelworks, machine plants and glass-factories employed over a million men, women and children. Flanders remained mainly agricultural apart from the cotton and linen mills around Ghent, and the thriving port of Antwerp; but an enormous number of Flemish poor took trains each day to work in the Walloon areas. This enormous and uneducated labour force was at first, as in England, totally unprotected from exploitation, on the grounds that only long hours and low wages could keep the employers solvent in the face of cut-throat competition. But the social concern that led England to develop a body of factory legis-lation by 1844, in defiance of current *laissez-faire* theories, was not felt in Belgium. Even after the revelations of the 1846 inquiry into the state of the poor, very little was done. Children, like men and women, worked long hours, factories were built without thought of hygiene or of safety, houses were slum dwellings; diet consisted

mostly of potatoes. For a long time the poor lived in an atmosphere of dull and brutish resignation, brilliantly registered in the drawings of Vincent Van Gogh, who spent three years as a lay preacher in the mining area of the Borinage. Karl Marx, who also spent three years in Belgium, made few recruits there,[5] and the French socialist thinkers mainly influenced Belgium's young bourgeois radicals. But in 1857 a group of Ghent weavers joined together in a 'brotherly society' that gradually developed into the Flemish Socialist party. Three years later, socialist Caesar de Paepe and radical Liberal Paul Janson founded *Le Peuple*, which became the mouthpiece of the Belgian branch of the First Socialist International after this organization was created in London in 1864. Socialist cells were established in industrial centres such as Ghent, Brussels and Verviers, but joint action was inevitably hampered by the language question.

During 1867 strikes broke out in the collieries of Charleroi and the Borinage. Eighteen men were shot down, and indignation led to mass rallies. In the same year, workers' unions were recognized, on condition that they concerned themselves only with mutual aid. Groups and associations soon proliferated, many of them copying Ghent's co-operative bakery *Vooruit* (Forward) founded in 1873 by Edward Anselle on the lines of the Rochdale co-operative pioneers. Workers' shops, cafés, bakeries, breweries, pharmacies and hospitals spread like wildfire through the industrial towns, and in 1885 Flemish and Walloon delegates from about sixty of them met at the Cygne tavern in Brussels' Grand'Place to found Belgium's *Parti Ouvrier Belge* (the Belgian Labour Party) with a young worker called Louis Bertrand at its head. For a long time members were more concerned with material well-being than with ideology, so that their party was essentially a federation of benefit societies with few true political groups.[6] They advocated public ownership of the basic means of production, but believed in private property. They disliked the Church's wealth but insisted, especially in the Flemish areas, that men's beliefs were their own private affair so long as the working class stood together against the capitalists. The *Maison du Peuple* (the Workers' Centre) in Brussels even had a portrait of Christ, 'the first socialist', in a main room. The party's main aims were free universal education, the legalization of trade unions, restriction of women's and children's labour, shorter working hours, employers' liability for accidents, the suppression of indirect taxes and the introduction of an income tax. Theoretically the party was republican, but workers were far from revolutionaries. Indeed, they raised their voteless voices in support of the middle-class progressive Liberal campaign for universal suffrage.

Liége, already boasting a long reputation as *la cité ardente* or the violent city, and strongly influenced by French radicalism, found this too moderate and urged workers to violence. In 1885 the miners of Charleroi came out on strike for a ten-hour day; glassworkers near Seraing destroyed plant and raised the red flag, and the revolt spread until Hainaut province was put under martial law. Troops, and later the law courts, showed no mercy, and the embittered workers marched in thousands on Brussels. Public opinion was on the side of law and order; but a fresh inquiry revealed such appalling conditions, including illhealth, illiteracy and child labour, that Catholic ministries began a series of reforms that continued over the next twenty years and included guaranteed minimum wages, workers' housing, old-age pensions, sickness and accident insurance, the Sunday rest day and the banning of nightwork for women and children. Trade unions gained substantial rights in 1898, but were not fully legalized until as late as 1921.

In the meantime the franchise still rested on a restricted property qualification, so that only 137,000 could vote out of a population which now totalled over six millions. To put teeth into its demand for universal suffrage, the *Parti Ouvrier Belge* launched a general strike in 1893. Twenty workers lost their lives, but after a week the cabinet surrendered and passed a law decreeing that all males over twenty-five should not only have the right but be required to vote. But generous plural votes were awarded to the educated classes. However, in 1894 Socialist members entered parliament for the first time with 28 seats; the Liberal vote plummeted to 14 and was never to rise again to first place: and a floodtide began for the Catholics, who won 104 seats.

The rise of socialism also made another mark on political life. Some of the older Catholics, like Charles Woeste, still preferred the virtue of charity to that of social justice; but younger Catholics were inspired by the ideals of Christian Democracy and set out to attract Catholic workers away from socialism, soon encouraged by the papal encyclical *Rerum Novarum*. Under the leadership of the Abbé Pottier of Liége and of Arthur Verhaegen, their *Ligue Démocratique Belge* encouraged Catholics to associate in benefit societies often modelled on the medieval craft guilds. The League's political programme aimed at protection of workers through legislation, and was very similar to that of the Socialists. The first Christian Democrats were elected to parliament in 1894, and joined forces with the young middle-class Catholics Jules Renkin and Henri Carton de Wiart, who were working for universal suffrage, compulsory education for all, conscription and a progressive income tax. From 1906 onwards the Primate of Belgium, Cardinal Mercier, was able to give them some support.

At first the Christian Democrats favoured the Catholic idea of 'vertical' trade unions common to workers and employers; but this was soon abandoned, and Catholic unions as well as co-operatives spread in the wake of the Socialist models. They made little impact in the great Walloon industrial centres, but succeeded well in small towns and in the countryside. Outstandingly successful was the *Boerenbond* or Peasants' League, centred in the Flemish areas, which organized rural savings banks, mutual aid and co-operatives for buying and selling of farm produce and fertilizers. It also became a powerful pressure group for agricultural protection. Like other co-operatives, it was helped by subsidies as its electoral influence grew.

All these movements, however, continued to arouse the deep distrust of the conservative wing of the Catholic party. At the same time the Socialists under a brilliant parliamentary orator, Emile Vandervelde, fostered an increasingly tumultuous parliamentary life, marked also by a series of big strikes and outbursts of anti-clericalism. The social struggle was again further complicated by the emergence of a small, passionately pro-Flemish Christian

Democrat group led by the Abbé Daens. This outraged all other Catholics by its indiscipline and its class polemics; it was condemned by the Church before it had achieved any political importance; but it was a sign of the times.

THE FLEMISH MOVEMENT

Although the rivalry between Flemings and French speakers was medieval in its origins, it had been submerged for centuries. The rural populations of Flanders, poor, submissive and politically null, had continued to speak Flemish after the sixteenth-century split from their Dutch co-linguists, without benefit of schools or books. Deprived of its backbone of grammar, the language had degenerated from its great medieval strength into a jumble of local dialects, scarcely comprehensible to the educated Dutchmen who ruled Belgium after 1815. By establishing schools in their language, William of the Netherlands was the first to rescue the culturally downtrodden Flemings; but they hated him for his Protestantism and for his favours to his own compatriots. After 1830, the swing away from all forms of 'hollandization' favoured French as the sole language of the constitution, of parliamentary debates and of public administration, despite the principle of free choice of language. Moreover, all educated Flemings preferred to speak French – which had been the language of the court and of the administration for centuries, even under Austrian rule.

Gradually, however, the Romantic movement in Europe began to spread its doctrines of respect for racial culture. Under its influence an Antwerp citizen (of French blood), Hendrik Conscience, began a revival of Flemish literature with historical novels modelled on Sir Walter Scott and Victor Hugo. A group of philologists led by Jan-Frans Willems studied Flemish history, medieval literature and folk legends, and began to claim for Flemish the equality that the law in theory acknowledged. In 1856 a Catholic minister, De Decker, set up a commission which soon asked that all official publications should be translated into Flemish; that law officials, army officers and diplomats should be able to use Flemish; and that Flemish should be the sole language of instruction for primary and secondary schools in Flanders. The commission's recommendations horrified the Liberals, who drew most of their own strength from the Walloon provinces and were not sympathetic to Flemish claims, which they considered an additional Catholic threat to the unity and cohesion of the young State. In their eyes the Flemish masses had been dangerously cut off, through their ignorance of the French language, from the ideals of the French Revolution which had so deeply influenced Belgium's constitution. In addition, the Flemish élite who had spoken French for centuries intended to give their children the fully French education they themselves had received. The colleges of the Jesuits and other Catholic teaching Orders also wished to continue using French as their only language of instruction.

But the agitation spread widely under the leadership of Jan Van Rijswijk of Antwerp, and successive Catholic ministries acknowledged the justice of the Flemish claims. In 1873 Flemish was made obligatory in criminal trials in the Flemish areas; and a few years later the same ruling was applied to all administrative affairs throughout Flanders. In 1883 Flemish was made a compulsory subject in Flemish secondary schools; a Royal Flemish Academy of Languages and Literature was founded at Ghent in 1886; by 1898 Flemish became the second official Belgian language and the king's oath, the coinage, and all public inscriptions became bilingual.

These measures increasingly disturbed the Walloons who until then had dominated the administration; but the quarrel raged mainly within the Flemish provinces between the Flemish-speaking patriots, nicknamed the *Flamingants*, and the Flemish *Fransquillons* who gave their first loyalty to French culture and were regarded by the Flamingants as traitors to their own race. Politically the Flamingants were naturally most numerous in the Catholic Party, but in 1911 the Catholic Frans Van Cauwelaert, the Liberal Louis Franck and the Socialist Camille Huysmans jointly organized a great petition for the creation of a Flemish university at Ghent, claiming that the under-privileged status of the Flemish language penalized Flemings economically and politically. Their attempt failed, but it illustrated the complex cross-currents which from now on were to dominate the Belgian scene.

57

In striking contrast to the narrowness of Belgium's domestic rivalries, industrially the country could and did think big. By the end of the nineteenth century Belgium ranked, despite her small size, among Europe's foremost exporters. Leopold himself gave a great lead to this activity; in his later years he not only raised capital in any way he could to develop the Congo, but also maintained financial interests that were literally world-wide. He gathered round him men like the banker Edouard Empain, who built the Paris underground, railroads in Russia, a tramway system for Cairo and the entire new city of Heliopolis in Egypt; Ernest Solvay, who developed one of Europe's biggest chemical industries and endowed the Solvay Institute in Brussels for the social and economic sciences; Emile Francqui, soldier, explorer and financier, a pioneer of Congolese industrial development; the engineer Jean Jadot, builder of the Pekin-Hankow railroad; and Alfred Thys, who, like Jadot, gave his name to an industrial town of the Congo. Belgian locomotives, railway tracks, tramlines, gas, electrical and coal-mining plant and steelworks combines could be found from Siam to Spain and from Russia to South America.

At home, though a great deal of poverty still existed, and compulsory schooling for Belgian children only became law in 1914, some of the educational pioneering done in wealthy communes had won European recognition – particularly the Froebel-type kindergartens and Charles Buls' model schools in Brussels. In the arts Belgium also produced a series of outstanding names, including the Liége composer César Franck, the painter James Ensor and the decorator-architects Horta and Van de Velde, who launched the vogue for Art Nouveau successfully throughout Europe.[7] Chief among Flemish-language writers were the priest, Guido Gezelle, whose lyric poems were as gothic in spirit as Flemish primitive art, Pol de Mont, Stijn Streuvels and the essayist and critic August Vermeylen, founder of *Van Nu en Straks* (Of Today and Tomorrow), a literary journal paralleled by the French-language *Jeune Belgique*. Paradoxically, Belgium's leading French-language writers were all Flemish; among them were Charles de Coster who wrote legendary stories of the wily, good-humoured resistance of Tyl Uilenspiegel against sixteenth-century Spanish tyranny, novelist Camille Lemonnier and the symbolist poet Emile Verhaeren. They all, like most Belgian writers of the time, extolled the past and present glories of their native land, while Nobel prizewinner Maurice Maeterlink wrote mystical plays in which his exquisite characters moved dreamlike towards inexplicable doom.

Despite the generally low level of wages and the extremely light taxation of the rich, the material conditions of the poor were from now on increasingly alleviated by the immense network of Socialist or Catholic activities that affected the workers' well-being throughout his life. They included not only the producers' and consumers' co-operatives and the benefit societies but even milk for babies, meals, shoes, medical examination and seaside holidays for school children, often run through the societies with the help of local Socialist or Catholic communes. The Socialist party also provided funds to finance strikes, a central Workers' Educational Organization and even a *Banque Belge du Travail* (Workers' Bank). From 1900 the Second Socialist International made its headquarters in the Maison du Peuple in Brussels, and was run by the Antwerp deputy Camille Huysmans.

While Belgium continued profoundly absorbed in her own affairs, the war clouds were gathering. In January 1904 Leopold returned from Germany secretly appalled by Wilhelm II's offer to create the medieval Duchy of Burgundy for Belgium, complete with French Artois and the French Ardennes, in return for Belgian co-operation in a war against France. Just before he died, five years later, the old King had the satisfaction of at last seeing the system of military service by lottery (with paid replacements for rich young men who drew unlucky numbers) replaced by conscription of one son from each family. But full military service only began in 1913, too late to make any real difference when Germany suddenly presented her ultimatum on 2 August 1914, demanding the right to cross Belgium into France. Belgium refused; France and Great Britain declared themselves bound by the 1839 guarantees of Belgium's inviolability; and once more the country became a battleground for European war.

5   Wars and languages

THE BELGIAN ARMY was too recently formed and trained to present any effective check against the German invasion. Within two months it had fallen back to a narrow strip of West Flanders between the river Yser and the French frontier, but King Albert and his troops were never dislodged from this last bit of Belgian territory throughout the four years' war that followed. Belgium's refusal to allow the German forces free passage through Belgian territory (which slowed down the German plan for a lightning swoop into France); its valiant if hopeless military resistance; and its hardships under occupation gave the country a world-wide reputation for courage and virtue, blotting out the criticism it had unfairly borne a few years before against misrule in King Leopold's Congo. King Albert, who had succeeded to the throne in 1909, became revered abroad as the symbol of resistance against unfair attack. His tentative negotiations with Germany for a separate peace were little known, came to nothing, and did not tarnish his legend as the heroic Soldier-King.[1]

On the outbreak of the war the Catholic cabinet transformed itself into an all-party government by co-opting Paul Hymans to represent the Liberals and Emile Vandervelde for the Socialists. During the retreat to the Yser, ministers left for Sainte Adresse near Le Havre in France, and there carried on such government as they could, without the King, but in co-operation with an international Commission for Relief in Belgium directed by the Americans under Herbert Hoover.

German exploitation of the Belgian heavy industries led to extensive strikes, the removal of industrial plant to Germany and, from

1916 onwards, to the deportation of some 160,000 workers. Huge fines were imposed on the population for its refusal to co-operate. Raw materials and food were requisitioned; and Belgium only managed to avoid severe malnutrition owing to the combined efforts of Britain, who allowed food for Belgium through the naval blockade, and to neutral diplomats such as the United States Minister to Belgium, Brand Whitlock, and his Spanish and Dutch counterparts, who continued to channel relief supplies after America declared war on Germany in April 1917. Attempts to bring Belgium to her knees by acts of terrorism soon lapsed, though hundreds of civilians suffered deaths less spectacular than those of Nurse Edith Cavell and of Belgian war heroine Gabrielle Petit; but clandestine newspapers such as *La Libre Belgique* (Free Belgium) helped to keep morale unshaken.

In an attempt to foster disunity the Germans took up the quarrel between Flemings and Walloons. 'Sire, there are no Belgians; you reign over two peoples,' writer Jules Destrée had told King Albert; and most Flemings took the same line, opposing the moderates who tried to argue that 'Fleming or Walloon are merely first names, but our family name is Belgian'. Many Flemings wanted administrative separation of the Flemish provinces from the rest of Belgium; some advocated links with their co-linguists in Holland; and a few sought union of some kind with Germany, mother of their own Low German speech. Nobody was satisfied with the Belgian State, and many would have agreed with the extremist *Vlaamsche Post* when it said in 1916, 'for eighty-five years Belgium has been the vampire of Flanders'. The great majority of Flemings preferred to settle accounts with the Walloons after the war, and resented the German intrusion into their private quarrels. But a small number, known as Activists, readily accepted German help.

One commonly agreed aim was to create a Flemish university at Ghent. This the Governor-General von Bissing decreed in March 1916, deporting world-famous historian Henri Pirenne and other university teachers because of their opposition. During the same period, Activist propaganda told the war-weary soldiers in the Yser trenches that it was unnatural for Flemish patriots to be allied with

France, against whom their ancestors had so often struggled. French-language officers added to this resentment by their mishandling of Flemish troops. In February 1917 the Activists set up an embryo separatist government in Ghent, called the Council of Flanders, but the Germans dissolved it. A year later the Germans themselves divided Belgium into two administrative units centred at Brussels and at Namur, but the burgomasters and the communes refused to recognize the new division. Attempts by the Activists to recruit public support in Brussels and in Flemish towns led to counter-rallies condemning them; they had made virtually no recruits when the German collapse began in the summer of 1918, and eventually they fled, either to Germany or into Holland. That September the Belgian army shared the Allied offensive. On 11 November, when the armistice was signed, the Belgians were at Ghent and the British at Mons, while farther south French and Americans were pushing into the region of the Sambre and Meuse rivers. Eleven days later King Albert and Queen Elisabeth entered Brussels with Belgian and Allied troops, among scenes of wild enthusiasm.

RECONSTRUCTION AND THE PEACE SETTLEMENT
The seventh of President Wilson's famous Fourteen Points of January 1918 had said that Belgium must not only be evacuated by Germany but 'restored'. This the Belgians took to mean that they would be paid indemnities. They expected much of the Versailles Peace Conference, but without waiting for it they began a ferocious effort to rebuild their collapsed economy. Relatively speaking, their losses in human life were light, with 36,000 killed and as many more gravely wounded; but factories had been systematically dismantled and heavy industrial plant smashed or removed; railways had been torn up and bridges dynamited during the German retreat; more than 100,000 houses were destroyed as well as schools, churches and other public buildings (some of them architectural jewels like the thirteenth-century Cloth Hall of Ypres); the famous library of Louvain University had been burned down; some of the best farmland was now flooded or trampled into mud, and more than half the country's livestock was lost.

Once the most urgent needs were taken in hand, parliament prepared new elections. It was evident that the conservatism brought back by the exiled Catholic ministers was out of key with the democratic aspirations that had developed during the war. On the other hand all Catholics, as well as Liberals, were now very much afraid of the godless Bolsheviks who were spreading their anti-Christian, anti-capitalist doctrines from Russia, inducing the Socialists to polish up their Marxism and raise their own claims.

In the elections of 1919 plural voting was abandoned for full universal male suffrage. Proportional representation, first introduced in 1899, and compulsory voting were both maintained. Seventy Socialists were returned to Parliament, as well as 73 Catholics and 34 Liberals. Together they set up an all-party government, which voted a series of social laws including low-cost housing schemes, an eight-hour day, complete liberty for trade unions, compulsory insurance for old age, a progressive income tax, and death duties. The old quarrel on education was partially appeased by the application of a law voted in 1914, granting equal eligibility for state subsidies to all schools.

When the Versailles negotiations began, Belgium was quickly given 2,500 million gold francs in reparations. Later, Belgians were promised a thirty-year indemnity from Germany, as well as supplies of coal, machinery and cattle. Like everybody else Belgium felt justified in squeezing Germany hard. Neither the British nor anyone else listened to Lloyd George when he doubted whether it was sensible 'to treat Germany like a cow from which to extract milk and beef at the same time'. But later Belgium and the other Allies faced the fact that Germany simply could not pay. To a large extent it was Belgian capital abroad that helped the country withstand its war losses – except for the vast holdings confiscated in Russia.

At Versailles the neutrality clause of the old 1839 treaty was abandoned, so that Belgium could safeguard her defences by military alliances as freely as any other sovereign country. But Belgium's bid to protect both military and economic interests by acquiring Dutch Limburg and Zeeland Flanders, around the Meuse and the Scheldt respectively, resulted in nothing but a revival of ill-feeling between the two neighbours. Belgians vainly hoped to recover the half of Luxembourg they had reluctantly lost in 1839, but an economic union between the two was signed on 25 July 1921. This still remains in force, the two territories being considered a single unit as regards customs and excise duties; the Belgian franc is also the official currency of the Grand Duchy. Belgium's only territorial gains were a small ex-German area east of Liége including Eupen and Malmédy, and in Africa, a League of Nations mandate over the former German territories of Rwanda and Urundi north of Lake Tanganyika. Exercising her new right to make alliances, Belgium signed a military pact with France in 1920, despite domestic opposition from anti-French Flemings. Plans for a Belgian military agreement with Great Britain similar to that with France came to nothing; but Britain gave Belgium some satisfaction at Locarno in 1925, when a mutual non-aggression agreement was signed between Germany, France, Belgium, Britain and Italy.

REVIVAL AND DEPRESSION

In the early post-war years the Socialist party was powerful and popular; but it began to lose its appeal through the excesses of its extremists – some of whom broke away in 1923 to form the Belgian Communist party – and partly because of the country's financial troubles. A first coalition between the Christian-Democrat wing of the Catholic party and the Socialists in 1925 sank in a morass of inflation and had to give way to an all-party cabinet under the banker Emile Francqui after the national debt had swollen to crisis point. Devaluation and other drastic reforms restored stability by the end of 1926, and power passed to the conservative Catholics and Liberals who held office, in a series of shifting coalitions, for the next eight years.

A period of material prosperity followed the stabilization of the franc. Traditional exports revived, while new industries sprang up, some of them centring round Congo produce such as copper, coffee and palm oil. Workers' wages were pegged to the cost of living. The Albert Canal was begun, to link Liége and Antwerp without passing through Dutch territory. But at the end of 1929 came the

64

Wall Street crash, sparking off a world-wide depression and return to protectionism. Absorbed in a recurrence of bitter strife between Flemings and Walloons, the government was slow to react to its profoundest economic crisis until unemployment became widespread, strikes broke out and there was a flight of capital. After the classic deflationary policies, including fiercely-resented wage reductions, had been tried the King called in the vice-governor of the National Bank, Paul van Zeeland. Leading a tripartite cabinet he devalued the franc once more, lowered interest rates and launched public works. Unemployment figures dropped within a year by two-thirds, helped by the upturn in international trade; and in 1936 the budget was balanced.

THE FLEMISH QUESTION

After the war popular resentment against the extremist Flemish minority spilled over all too easily against Flemish claims in general. Activists were tried and imprisoned; ringleaders were given commuted death sentences. Soon a new movement calling itself the Front party came to the fore, led by exiles and Flemish ex-soldiers, who complained that reprisals against the Activists had been excessive, as the condemned men were after all sincere Flemish patriots. The Front party itself was neither pro-German nor pro-Dutch, but it opposed the Belgian State which it accused of being French in its origins, inspired by French ideals and contemptuous of the Flemish nation. The pact of 1920 with France was feared to be the thin end of a wedge leading to the disappearance of Flemish language and culture. Frontists had written to President Wilson in May 1919, pleading that 'you may so far interest yourself in the pitiful case of the oppressed Flemings . . . as to cause an independent inquiry to be made into the Flemish question . . . to satisfy yourself that the new order of things in Europe is incompatible with a continuation of the wilful oppression of that race within the Kingdom of Belgium'.[2] During the 1920s political and emotional agitation grew, stimulated by village priests who infused the movement with a mystical and religious appeal. They invented a powerful new slogan, in the symbol of the cross:

A

V V K

V

meaning *Alles voor Vlaanderen, Vlaanderen voor Kristus* – all for Flanders, Flanders for Christ. Their sense of local patriotism was even greater than that of most Belgians. 'I first belong to my village,' wrote a supporter, 'and then to my small country, Flanders.'[3] Their patriotic song was *The Lion of Flanders* and their emblem a black lion on a yellow ground. They scorned the Belgian flag and the Belgian anthem the *Brabançonne*, and disliked even more the *Marseillaise*, the Socialists' favourite hymn. To them the French language was 'a vehicle for microbes' and France a degenerate country dominated by freethinking and godlessness. The quarrel flared up unpleasantly at the end of 1928 when August Borms, a leading wartime Activist, was elected to parliament for Antwerp with 83,000 votes while still serving a prison sentence. By 1929 eleven Frontists sat in the Chamber of Representatives, though the party soon splintered into rival groups.

After a general amnesty in 1929, good relations were patched up for the centenary celebrations of 1930, when the Flemings had the satisfaction of seeing Ghent University made a completely Flemish-language foundation. Two years later, despite a new financial crisis, a Catholic-Liberal coalition attempted a thoroughgoing settlement of the language problem, which had now had a disturbed political life for more than fifty years. The country was to be divided into two separate regions, by official recognition of the language frontier – which had scarcely changed throughout Belgium's entire history. This historic boundary was carefully traced from Menin to Tongeren, cutting through some of the nine provinces but safeguarding the rights of the mother-tongue of each district. North of this line only Flemish was to be used in all branches of public administration, as also in schools, the army and the lawcourts. Similarly, French alone was to be used in the Walloon area, while Brussels was to be officially bilingual. In all Belgian schools the first modern language taught was to be the language of the other region. At the same time Louvain University divided itself into Flemish and French-language sections, and the University of Brussels instituted courses in Flemish.

This legislation penalized those Flemings who wished to remain French-speaking, and Walloons who disliked the obligation to learn Flemish. But it protected Flemings from the bullying of French-language administrators that had undoubtedly occurred in the past. Above all, it meant that a Flemish child could continue his studies to university level without the extra difficulty of mastering another language; this, the Flemings felt, had given a built-in advantage to the Walloons in acquiring degrees and diplomas and consequently the best jobs. No longer, they hoped, would Flemings be condemned always to the second-best places; no longer would they be made to feel second-class citizens even in their own region. The laws were accepted as a practical solution for a problem that had become explosive. Despite the settlement – or perhaps partly because of it – relations between Flemings and Walloons remained tense.

THE ROYAL FAMILY

Another event that marked national life during these difficult years was the sudden death of King Albert on 17 February 1934 after a climbing accident in the Meuse valley. He had been deeply respected by most of his people, including dissident Flemings as well as republican-minded Socialists. Six days later his thirty-three-year-old son took the oath as Leopold III. He too was to share personal tragedy only eighteen months later, when his car crashed during a holiday near Küssnacht in Switzerland, killing his Swedish-born wife Astrid. Queen Astrid like King Albert had been widely popular in both parts of the country, and like him had helped make the monarchy a valuable rallying point among the quarrels that sometimes seemed likely to split the country apart. Indeed, from the moment she had first arrived in her new country in 1926, a solitary white figure at the bows of a white ship appearing through the mists of Antwerp harbour, Astrid had charmed the Belgian people. By some effortless secret she seemed to know how to mix magic with approachability in a way that delighted both the popular love of

THE LINGUISTIC AREAS

⊙ National capital

○ Provincial capital

– · – Provincial frontiers

Flemish

French

Bi-lingual (French-Flemish)

German speaking with protected French speaking minority

Flemish speaking with protected French speaking minority

French speaking with protected Flemish speaking minority

French speaking with protected German speaking minority

0   40 M

0   70 KM

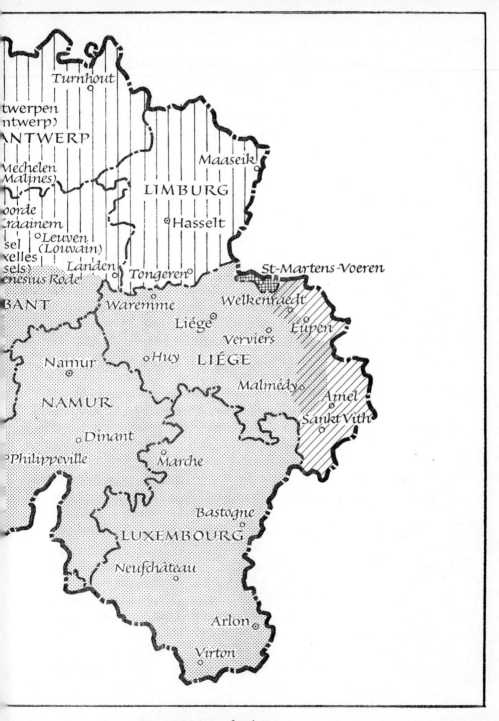

Linguistic map of Belgium

princes and Belgium's democratic spirit. Perhaps the fact that she arrived knowing neither French nor Flemish had something to do with her appeal. No doubt her early death increased her legend; but twenty-five years later she was still remembered with fervent affection. Some Belgian cottages even now have photographs of Queen Astrid with a lamp burning in front, as in front of pictures of the saints.

REXISM

At the time of the world economic crisis Hitler had established himself in Germany, and the totalitarian ideas preached by him and Mussolini were making headway in Europe. In 1935 a twenty-nine-year-old ex-student of Louvain University named Léon Degrelle started a Belgian movement in favour of his own brand of authoritarianism flavoured with Christianity, which he called Rexism from the name Christus Rex (Christ the King). By no means a profound thinker, but with unrivalled powers of invective and a flair for publicity, Degrelle began to attract to himself the type of people who in other countries responded to Fascism: the insecure and the embittered, people on their way up who had lost their savings and their prospects, or those who feared to be caught in a new recession. Degrelle attacked first the Catholics and then Socialist and Liberal leaders who were responsible, he said, for recent business crashes; unfolding endless stories of trickery, he promised to purge corruption and to restore the simple virtues of family life and of local patriotism. His party won twenty-two seats in the 1936 elections, most of them at the expense of the Walloon right-wing Catholics.

Outdone by Degrelle in condemnation of the financial oligarchies, the Socialist party intensified its noisy demands for the overthrow of the capitalist state, while securing whatever material benefits it could from legislation or strikes. Typical of the Socialists of the time was the young Paul-Henri Spaak, who almost overnight in March 1935 stopped demanding 'a human torrent sweeping away everything in its path' and joined van Zeeland's 'government of bankers' as Minister of Transport. Soon afterwards, the Popular Front formed in France; French workers won considerable social benefits while in Belgium workers had felt little of the economic recovery. Socialists were losing heavily to the Communists. They started a strike movement, and Degrelle campaigned against the entire left, proclaiming 'Rex or Moscow'. He allied with a Flemish extremist movement sympathetic to Nazism, called the *Vlaamsch National Verbond* or VNV (Flemish Nationalist Party), and in 1937 was holding monster meetings on the lines of Hitlerite rallies. When Degrelle presented himself as a candidate in an April by-election in Brussels, van Zeeland himself stood against him, denouncing him as a Fascist. Degrelle was crushingly defeated, and the Rexists never recovered their sudden popularity. In 1939 only four of them won parliamentary seats.

In the meantime, small Flemish movements inspired by Nazism sprang up, such as the Verdinaso group, whose programme included the subjugation of the French-language provinces. More important was the VNV. This movement aimed at uniting the Flemish provinces with the Netherlands in a separatist state, and at making Brussels a unilingual Flemish city. In 1936 it won sixteen seats in parliament, mostly at the expense of the Catholics. To meet this challenge the Catholic party in the same year split into French and Flemish-language sections.

In the Walloon areas a separatist movement also arose, in reaction against the fear of being outnumbered by Flemings. It had no electoral success, but a Walloon Socialist proposal for constitutional revision separating Belgium into a federal state won 73 votes.

REARMAMENT AND POLITICAL STALEMATE

The 1936 upturn in the country's finances did not last. After voting a forty-hour week, a week's annual paid holiday for certain workers and compulsory sickness and unemployment insurance for all, the van Zeeland government was forced to resign office in October 1937 over a bank scandal. A new government was eventually formed by Paul-Henri Spaak, who had already held the ministry of Foreign Affairs as well as the Transport ministry under van Zeeland. While the budget deficit swelled once more, the international storm clouds were gathering.

In 1933 Germany had left the League of Nations, and three years later Hitler reoccupied the left bank of the Rhine in defiance of the Locarno Treaty. Just before this, Belgium had renounced her own 1920 military pact with France because of mounting opposition from the Flemings. Later in 1936 the Belgian all-party government withdrew their country, on King Leopold's advice, from the shreds of the shattered Locarno pact, in favour of a policy of independence. The British and French governments officially acknowledged Belgium's return to freedom of action on 24 April 1937, but maintained the offers of aid they had made to Belgium at Locarno without asking for any reciprocity. In October of the same year Germany also pledged herself to respect the integrity of Belgian territory. So Belgium again stood on the same footing as in 1914, with her independence guaranteed by her three powerful neighbours; this time, however, her neutrality was self-imposed.

Parliamentary government was in a low state. Ever since single-party government had ended with World War I, unstable coalitions had succeeded each other, often dissolving for no good reason, leaving weeks of parliamentary paralysis, while prospective prime ministers tried to meet the demands of the many different sub-groups within the parties, and to fuse their conflicting desires into something like a coherent policy. As King Leopold complained, since the first world war there had been no clear majorities, but each cabinet contained a 'dosage' of every political shade of opinion within the parties, and it was to these factions that ministers felt responsible rather than to the country as a whole; so that, as Leopold said, 'disorder and confusion prevailed when the country needed firm government'.[4] Hitler's invasion of Austria, the Czech crisis and the Munich agreement of 1938 between Germany, Italy, France and Great Britain, increased Belgium's desperate wish to keep out of the European vortex. In 1939 the cost of national defence rose to one-fifth of the total state budget. But parliament seemed unable or unwilling to abandon its inner quarrels; a weak tripartite cabinet under a Catholic lawyer, Hubert Pierlot, was just emerging from yet another impasse when, on 3 September 1939, World War II began.

1 Ypres, Wipers to soldiers of World War I and Ieper to its Flemish inhabitants, lost its thirteenth-century Cloth Hall to the Kaiser's shells, but has now been fully restored.

2 A part of Brussels' historic skyline, dominated by the graceful spire of the fifteenth-century Town Hall and the obese dome of the nineteenth-century Law Courts.

CAPVT PRIMVM.

IN principio creauit Deus cælum & terram. Terra autem
erat inanis & vacua: & tene-
bræ erant super faciem abyssi:
& spiritus Dei ferebatur su-
per aquas. Dixitq; Deus, Fiat lux. & facta est
lux. Et vidit Deus lucem quod esset bona: &
diuisit lucem à tenebris. Appellauitq; lucem
diem, & tenebras noctem. Factumq; est vespere
& mane dies vnus. Dixit quoque Deus, Fiat
firmamentú in medio aquarum, & diuidat a-
quas ab aquis. Et fecit Deus firmamentum,
diuisitq; aquas, quæ erant sub firmamento, ab
his quæ erant super firmamentum. Et factum
est ita. Vocauitq; Deus firmamentum, cælum: &
factum est vespere, & mane dies secundus.
Dixit verò Deus, Congregentur aquæ quæ
sub cælo sunt, in locum vnum: & appareat ari-
da. Et factum est ita. Et vocauit Deus aridam,
terram: congregationesq; aquarum appellauit
maria. Et vidit Deus quod esset bonum. Et
ait, Germinet terra herbam virentem & facientem semen, & lignum pomiferú faciens fructú
iuxta genus suum, cuius semen in semetipso sit
super terram. Et factú est ita. Et protulit terra
herbam virentem, & facientem semen iuxta genus
suú, lignumq; faciens fructú, & habens vnum-
quodq; sementem secundú speciem suam. Et
vidit Deus quod esset bonum. Et factum est
vespere & mane dies tertius. Dixit autê Deus,
Fiant luminaria in firmamento cæli, & diui-
dant diem ac noctê, & sint in signa & têpora,
& dies & annos: Vt luceant in firmaméto cæli,
& illuminent terram. Et factum est ita. Fecitq;
Deus duo luminaria magna: luminare maius,
vt præesset diei: & luminare minus, vt præesset
nocti; & stellas. Et posuit eas Deus in firmaméto cæli, vt lucerent super terram. Et præessent
diei ac nocti, & diuiderent lucem ac tenebras.
Et vidit Deus quod esset bonum. Et factum est
vespere, & mane dies quartus. Dixit etiam
Deus, Producant aquæ reptile animæ viuentis,
& volatile super terram sub firmamento cæli.

3–5 Sixteenth-century Antwerp was a centre of learning and the arts. Here Christophe Plantin printed his polyglot Bible (left), and Abraham Ortelius' atlas of the then known world, *Typus Orbis Terrarum* (below). After peace was restored under the rulers Isabella and Albrecht, Flanders enjoyed a return of artistic splendour with such painters as the Breughels, Rubens and Van Dyck. A detail from a painting by Hendrik Staben (opposite, above) shows Albrecht and his wife Isabella in Rubens' studio.

6 Louis XIV at the siege of Namur, 1692; to set-piece operations such as this Louis invited his mistresses to enjoy the spectacle – at a suitable distance.

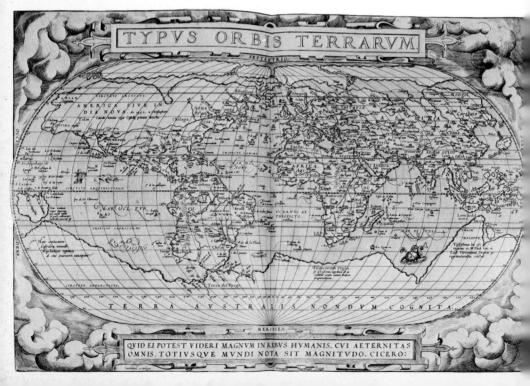

TYPVS ORBIS TERRARVM

QVID EI POTEST VIDERI MAGNVM IN REBVS HVMANIS, CVI AETERNITAS
OMNIS, TOTIVSQVE MVNDI NOTA SIT MAGNITVDO. CICERO.

7 William I of the Netherlands and the Englishman John Cockerill (above). William's financial support helped Lancashire-born Cockerill to make Belgian industry England's closest runner-up in early nineteenth-century Europe.

8 The annual procession of barefoot, hooded penitents at Veurne near Ostend continues a tradition influenced by sixteenth-century Spanish mysticism.

9 A seventeenth-century Belgian missionary, Father Louis Hennepin, accompanied the Frenchman La Salle in the exploration of North America. The picture opposite, from Hennepin's *New Discovery of America*, shows the murder of La Salle by two of his own men.

10–12 Leopold II, King of the
Belgians (left) whose acquisition
and exploitation of the Congo first
almost lost, and subsequently
gained, him a personal fortune. On
Leopold's initiative Henry Morton
Stanley (left, below), spent three
years opening up the area for trade,
hewing paths for roads and
railways through bush and forest.
Railways were needed for access to
the sea, because of cataracts near
the river mouth. Below: an early
locomotive at Stanleyville, 1905.

13 The Congo today is one of the
world's leading exporters of
copper. Opposite: electrolytic
refining at Luilu.

14 King Albert and Queen Elisabeth rode in triumph into Brussels at the head of Allied troops in November 1918 after four years of war. Beside them, representing his father, rode the future King George VI of England.

6   The King and the exiles

ON THE FIRST OF SEPTEMBER Germany invaded Poland, and two days later France and Great Britain declared war on Germany. Belgium immediately re-announced her neutrality, but began mobilization of her army of 650,000, resisting British and French pressure to be allowed to send troops into Belgium to share military preparations during the winter of 1939–40. The Belgians were understandably determined to avoid, if there was any possible chance of doing so, being once again Europe's battlefield.

For them, as for the rest of Europe, the next eight months were unnervingly quiet. In January of 1940 a German courier plane made a forced landing on Belgian territory; one of its pilots carried confidential papers, which he threw into a lighted stove as he was being questioned. A Belgian officer thrust his hand in the flames and drew them out, three parts burned: enough was legible to show that they were full German plans for the destruction of the Belgian army. Even so, for months afterwards nothing happened; then the phony war ended abruptly for Belgium in the early hours of 10 May, when German parachutists attacked the fort of Eben-Emael on Belgium's eastern border, and an air-raid over Evere aerodrome near Brussels destroyed half the country's tiny air force on the ground. The government immediately called on French and British aid, and rejected the German ultimatum – which in any case arrived four hours after the German bombs. The form of the German note echoed that of 1914: the Reich, it said, was forced to occupy Belgium in order to forestall imminent invasion by France and Britain. If Belgium resisted, this would risk the destruction of the country and the loss of independence.

Within three days Belgian troops were forced back to Belgium's Maginot Line running from Koningshoyckt near Antwerp to Wavre. Supreme Allied command was given to the French. While heavy fighting raged in these areas, a surprise thrust of panzer divisions began on 13 May in the Ardennes. Supported by artillery and air bombardment, the Germans easily reached the Meuse and pressed on towards the Channel ports in a wide sweep westwards, until they successfully cut off the three Allied armies from French and British forces farther south, around the Somme. Troops fought doggedly in an inevitable retreat; among civilians a panic flight began, but there was none of the fifth-columnist sabotage that helped the German advance in other countries. On 15 May the French commander ordered a retreat behind the Scheldt. To the north, the Dutch laid down their arms.

By 21 May the Germans had reached the Channel coast, and British and French attempts to re-establish contact with their armies on the Somme failed. A French plan for counter-attack under General Weygand dissolved as it became evident that the three armies in Belgium were encircled, and increasingly at the mercy of the German panzers and dive-bombers. By this time the roads were congested by refugees fleeing south in blind panic – before the end of the fighting over a million of them had escaped into France, and had almost paralysed troop movements in their flight. Formations of bombers continuously bombed and machine-gunned, and by 21 May it was obvious that the troops had little choice but surrender or escape. On the next day General Gort used an unexpected lull in the attack[1] to begin a withdrawal of British troops towards Dunkirk, while the French were already retreating to the south. The Belgians fought on tenaciously, but had nearly reached the limits of their endurance, as Leopold informed the French commander-in-chief on 26 May and as the British were well aware from previous warnings by the Belgian King. 'We are asking them to sacrifice themselves for us,' said Churchill in a private dispatch to Gort the next day, as British ships massed in Dunkirk harbour. He added, in an accompanying message to Admiral Keyes, British liaison officer with King Leopold, 'What can we do for him? Certainly we cannot serve

Belgium's cause by being hemmed in and starved out.' Leopold equally believed that he could no longer serve the Allied cause with his discouraged, ceaselessly bombed but still stubbornly fighting troops. All were well aware that military catastrophe was imminent. On the evening of 27 May Leopold decided to ask for an armistice, and told the French and British missions at his headquarters of his decision. The latter informed London, as the French informed General Weygand, but owing to breakdowns in communications the information was not successfully conveyed to the British and French troops in the field, who were now separated from each other and from the Belgians.

Whether Leopold gave his British and French allies sufficient notice before capitulating, and whether he did what he could to preserve their chances of cutting their losses, has been the subject of heated controversy both then and since. It was certainly clear well before 28 May that the three armies were encircled and could not hold out; Britain had first begun to assemble rescue boats on her south-east coast as early as 20 May,[2] and Leopold might have considered he should stop Belgian bloodshed even sooner. It is also clear that the men on the spot lived in an atmosphere of intense strain – short of supplies, often losing contact with their allies, ceaselessly strafed by low-swooping German planes and above all overwhelmed by the Germans' bewilderingly unexpected power and speed. It is easy for later critics to pass harsh judgments against Leopold on the basis of documents studied in quiet libraries. The most that can be said is that he might have shown more concern about whether his messages reached the Allies in the field, to inform them of action they knew to be inevitable.

In the meantime, from the English coast had arrived at Dunkirk an armada of over 850 vessels of every imaginable kind, from destroyers to small private boats manned by amateur sailors. This makeshift flotilla miraculously succeeded during the next few days in rescuing a quarter of a million British troops and more than 100,000 French. By 3 June this 'Operation Dynamo' was completed.

The last four of King Leopold's ministers had left in a British warship from Dunkirk on 25 May, *en route* to France via England.

Their pleas for the King to accompany them and continue the war from French soil had been in vain. As he told his soldiers in a proclamation informing them of his surrender on 28 May, he would not leave them in their misfortune. On the same day he wrote a letter to President Roosevelt, explaining the military reasons for his decision. To continue fighting, he said, would have exterminated both Belgian troops and refugees, without benefit to the Allies. He sent an identical letter to Pope Pius XII, and had a number of documents sent to the government in Paris, including the opinion of three eminent Belgian jurists justifying his action. After that he was silent on the capitulation question until after the end of the war.

The Fall of France

But the world was not silent. Winston Churchill on 28 May paid tribute to the bravery of the Belgian army, and added that no one should attempt to pass judgment on the action of the King of the Belgians. In Paris, however, on the same day, Paul Reynaud broadcast a blistering condemnation of Leopold. Reynaud, like Churchill later, overlooked the fact that Belgium had a right to expect British and French help by virtue of their commitment of 24 April 1937. On pressure from Reynaud, Belgian Premier Hubert Pierlot came to the microphone on the same day to reject Leopold's decision. He told Belgian officials that they were freed from their oath to obey the King, who was no longer in a position to reign, being under the control of foreigners. Pierlot said nothing to tone down Reynaud's recriminations, and in this way the French retained, temporarily at least, their cherished belief that their army was strong and had lost because it had been betrayed.

The Belgian cabinet had indeed disapproved, not of Leopold's military surrender, but of his decision to remain in Belgium. A week before the capitulation, Pierlot had written to the King, stressing the necessity on political grounds for Leopold to avoid capture, as this would dissociate Belgium from the Allied war effort. Most of the cabinet left for France; the four ministers who remained in Belgium after 18 May (Premier Pierlot, Foreign Minister Spaak, Minister of the Interior Arthur van der Poorten and Defence Minister

84

General Denis) argued every day with the King to persuade him to accompany them when the Belgian front fell. If he remained, they said, it would be virtually impossible to prevent the Germans from profiting by his presence, even against his will. Far from being a rallying point, Leopold would occupy a position contradictory to that of his government. It was true, they admitted, that King Albert also had refused to leave Belgian territory during the first world war to join his government in exile; but the difference was that Albert had continued fighting. They failed to shake the King's decision, however, and parted from him on very bad terms when they left on 25 May, while within Belgium Leopold withdrew completely from public life as a prisoner under German guard in the château of Laeken.

In France, Reynaud's broadcast condemning Leopold created an almost intolerable situation for the innumerable Belgian refugees, and for the hapless Belgian government. Cowed by Reynaud's anger, remembering their own recent disputes with the King, they outdid the French premier in their condemnation of Leopold. On 31 May, 89 Belgian deputies and 54 senators held an unofficial parliamentary session in Limoges, between Paris and Bordeaux, where they voted a resolution 'unanimously stigmatizing' the capitulation; some even demanded that Leopold should be deposed. Spaak spoke as harshly of the King as the rest; but he seemed to be the only one to suspect that Reynaud might be using Leopold as a scapegoat to cover France's desperate plight. At this time the British ambassador in Paris was telegraphing Churchill urging him to back up Reynaud's condemnation, as French ministers complained that British refusal to do so was leading to defeatism in France. On 4 June Churchill echoed Reynaud's story in the House of Commons, no doubt abandoning his hesitation now that the Belgian government itself had publicly condemned the King. He paid tribute to the 'brave, efficient' Belgian army; Sir Roger Keyes and others, soon including the United States ambassador to Brussels, Mr John Cudahy, actively defended Leopold; but the legend of his 'betrayal' was launched. Back in Brussels, Socialist Henri de Man, who was very close to Leopold during these days, said that the King 'seemed almost out of his senses, crying or suddenly rigidly controlling himself again; he suffered horribly in his pride'.

Soon the Allies had other things to think about. On 7 June German forces crossed the Somme, and a week later entered Paris. On 22 June Pétain signed an armistice with the Germans. Great Britain now faced an enemy victorious from Norway to the Spanish frontier. As the air battle raged that summer, Britain forgot about King Leopold; in any case, more from phlegmatic detachment than from good will, the British outcry against him had never struck the hysterical notes that had prevailed in France.

At home in Belgium there was universal condemnation of Pierlot's broadcast, and an outpouring of gratitude to Leopold for staying with them after stopping the agony of useless fighting. Messages of loyalty reached Laeken from all over the country, and not least from the refugees who, victimized by the angry French, were returning home as fast as they could. After the French collapse the Belgian ministers found themselves in complete disarray. Condemned by the Belgian people from whom they derived their authority, unwelcome to the Vichy government, they were swept from Paris to Poitiers to Limoges to Bordeaux and to Vichy, like the refugees they now were. Soon they wanted nothing so much as to return home. On 21 July, Pierlot expressed his hope that all Belgians would aim at national union around their King; and in an ironic *volte-face* the ministers did what Leopold had not done: they tried to negotiate an armistice with Germany, sending messages to Leopold asking for his co-operation, as was necessary under the constitution. But the King merely repeated that as a prisoner he could perform no political acts. Left completely to their own devices, most of the parliamentarians were back home by September. There, 74 of them sent a joint letter to the King, apologizing for the condemnation of Limoges. Their action was copied by a number of returning ministers. Others, however, had hastened to England. By the end of October Pierlot and Spaak had secretly crossed Spain and reached London, where they officially established themselves as the Belgian government-in-exile, and remained for the next four years as part of the international coalition against the Axis powers.

Although the Germans 'bought' rather than took (as in the first world war) finished articles and machinery, and later food and raw materials, they exercised more and more direct control, until they acquired a virtual stranglehold on industrial and agricultural production. By the time the Germans attacked the Soviet Union in June 1941, Belgium had lost more than half her rolling stock, and almost 2,000 locomotives; most of her coal, steel, textiles, diamonds, precious metals and foreign currency followed. Paper money came to mean so little that people returned to bartering all objects of value – real estate, paintings, furniture. The poor suffered severely as black market prices soared. Rickets and tuberculosis became alarmingly common among children.

By October 1940, 70,000 Belgians, mostly Jews, had already been deported; indeed, of Belgium's 80,000 Jewish population, only 1,500 survived the war. From March 1942 any men aged between eighteen and fifty, or unmarried women between eighteen and thirty-five could be forcibly recruited for work in Germany, and were often rounded up, in the streets. Almost half a million people had been deported before the end came; thousands of men hid in the Ardennes or in the Flemish Campine. All this was accompanied by ceaseless propaganda, in which the Rexists and the Flemish Nationalist VNV were ready collaborators. Degrelle led some Rexists to the Russian front. At home, as in World War I, the Germans made a deliberate effort to favour the Flemings, in order to undermine national unity – which was far more solid than in peacetime. Groups of Flemish SS were established, who swore allegiance to the Reich and wished to incorporate the Flemish provinces in it. But their excesses made them hated by the majority of their Flemish compatriots, who suffered as did other Belgians from increasing hardship. To express popular exasperation and hostility, over 200 small clandestine newspapers sprang up, denouncing the propaganda, the pillage, and the collaborators.

By nature turbulent and rebellious against authority, the Belgians developed a first-class resistance movement. They became so well organized that in 1942, according to Churchill's memoirs, they were

87

sending 80 per cent of the information received in London about German defences in the west. There were more than ten thousand agents at work, of whom three hundred had been parachuted in. Belgians also became supreme in Europe at successfully helping British and Allied soldiers and secret agents to escape.

Of the many resistance groups that sprang up spontaneously, three became outstanding. The *Mouvement national belge*, with recruits among the gendarmerie and the police, published one of the chief clandestine newspapers, as well as collecting information and directing sabotage. The *Front de l'indépendance* found recruits among all political parties and gradually became dominated by the communists. The *Légion belge* drew most of its strength from reserve officers. These movements, together with their smaller counterparts like the Liége Army of Liberation and the Antwerp White Brigade, were grouped in 1943 by the London government into the Secret Army, under Colonel Bastin of the *Légion belge*; but in practice they remained more or less autonomous. Among the recruits to the maquis in the Ardennes was the king's brother Charles, who lived in hiding for months. More and more as time went on, underground groups took reprisals against Germans and collaborators, particularly against those involved in recruiting forced labour. According to the Germans, 8,000 acts of sabotage occurred in 1943 alone.

On 6 June 1944, the BBC message 'King Solomon has put on his big wooden clogs' – one of the many transmitted to European resistance circuits and made deliberately fantastic to avoid their being spoken by accident – set off a larger-scale insurrection to coincide with the Allied invasion of the continent. But some of the best resistance work in the last stages of the war was the preservation of Belgium's key centres – notably the port of Antwerp – from destruction by the retreating Germans.[3]

Gradually, in all this upsurge of popular resentment against the Germans, a change developed in public attitudes towards the King. His enforced passivity under the occupation no longer corresponded with public feeling. In addition, the popular image of the solitary 'prisoner at Laeken', epitome of the 70,000 Belgian prisoners of war, was marred when on 6 December 1941 the Archbishop of Malines,

Cardinal van Roey, announced that on the previous 11 September Leopold had contracted a second marriage. Many disliked his choice – Mademoiselle Liliane Baels, a daughter of the Governor of West Flanders. Liberals and Socialists complained that the King's civil marriage had not preceded the religious rites, as the law of the land required. They wondered at the secrecy and delay in the announcement. Under Communist stimulus, criticism of the King grew, especially in the Walloon areas where, inevitably, his choice of a Flemish bride could not be popular.

Contact between King Leopold and the government-in-exile was virtually nil throughout the war, although the exiles now took every public opportunity to correct their early condemnation of their sovereign. In July 1941 the government published in London its official account of the events of 1940, ending with the words 'the King has shown himself to be the incarnation of a people which will not accept servitude'.

The Minister of Finance, Camille Gutt, and Minister of the Colonies, Albert de Vleeschauwer, had been among the first Belgians to arrive in London; throughout the war the government-in-exile put the wealth of the Congo into the Allied war effort. The production of tin, copper, zinc, industrial diamonds, palm oil, coffee and rubber soared in answer to the demands of war, and was of the utmost value. Congolese uranium was also used in atomic research.

Colonial troops from the Congo took part in the Abyssinian campaign. In England, Belgians were recruited into special units of the British forces: more than 700 joined the Royal Air Force; a Belgian section was formed in the Royal Navy; ships of the Belgian merchant navy had made for British ports in 1940; and Belgians manned a motorized brigade, including commandos and parachutists, which operated in Italy and Holland.

On 6 June 1944, when D-Day operations began, King Leopold was transferred by the Gestapo to Germany, and was later moved with his family to the Austrian village of Ströbl near Salzburg. He was released on 7 May 1945, by American troops under General Patch.

In the meantime, liberation had come to Belgium. On 3 September 1944, General Montgomery's troops crossed the Belgian frontier near Tournai in pursuit of the fleeing Germans; a few hours later the British Second Army (which included the Belgian Piron Brigade) entered Brussels. British and Canadian forces liberated Antwerp the next day with help from the Belgian resistance movement, while the United States First Army entered south-east Belgium, capturing the fortresses of Liége and Namur. Within four days the entire country was freed, and a *kermesse* followed such as Belgium had never seen. But the war was not yet over. During the winter Hitler's V-bombs fell in hundreds and did considerable damage in Liége and Antwerp, by now General Eisenhower's main port of supply. In December, moreover, the Germans made a major breakthrough in the Ardennes in an attempt to repeat the surprise encirclement of 1940. The Americans met von Rundstedt's forces in the narrow mountain roads near Bastogne on Christmas Day. Asked to surrender Bastogne, General McAuliffe, Commander of the US 101st Airborne Division, gave the famous one-word answer: 'Nuts!' Two months later the Battle of the Bulge was over, with heavy American and German losses. All fighting in Belgium then ceased, and the country shared in the world-wide rejoicings when at last, on 8 May 1945, peace returned to Europe.

7   Domestic discords

WHEN THE GOVERNMENT RETURNED home from its London exile in September 1944 the country was in a political and social turmoil which Pierlot, a tired and conservative-minded man, was ill-equipped to face. The general dislocation of normal life excluded any possibility of early elections; moreover, half a million Belgian workers and 60,000 prisoners of war were still in German hands. By common consent the cabinet was remodelled to include resistance leaders, among them two Communists; and a joint session of parliament appointed Prince Charles as Regent in the absence of King Leopold.

Together they set about four major tasks: to provide food and fuel; to revive the economy; to prevent inflation; and to restore law and order – including the purge of collaborators, against whom the public had begun to take action without waiting for legal trials. The Communists led the outcry against 'traitors' and against the black market, and encouraged members of the resistance movements to refuse to return to normal civil government. Pierlot tried to counter this restlessness by promising gradually to incorporate 40,000 resistance members into the army or the police, on condition that each individual at once gave up his arms. When he called for the compulsory surrender of arms by November 1944, strikes and riots broke out. Pierlot appealed to British troops to protect the government headquarters from attack, but four people were killed, and the subsequent indignation led to the downfall of his cabinet, as well as a swing of popular feeling away from the British in favour of the United States – which at that time was in any case vital to Belgium's recovery as a source of credit and a customer for the Congo's precious uranium deposits.

Outstanding to the 'London' government's credit, however, was the drastic action taken by the Finance Minister, Camille Gutt, within a month of the cabinet's return. By a series of decrees, this non-party monetary expert withdrew the Nazi-inflated currency from circulation, replacing it by a new note-issue printed beforehand in London. People who surrendered the old paper money did not immediately receive its full equivalent in the new; about 40 per cent of the total was converted into part of the national debt, at 3.5 per cent interest, and was only gradually allowed back into circulation. Together with the blocking of bank accounts and similar measures, this successfully stabilized the currency and also struck at war profits, including the raging black market. A few months later the food shortage was eased under an all-party government formed by Achille Van Acker in February 1945. With a well-fed population, freedom from inflation, resources from the Congo and valuable dollars earned from Allied forces for the still-continuing war, Belgian production was rapidly restored. Industrial plant had not been much damaged during the occupation, and the rapid German retreat had left little devastation in its wake; consequently the country quickly began to export goods essential to European reconstruction, particularly steel and machinery. Soon Belgium was thriving in a way unequalled by any other liberated country, deliberately relaxing controls in favour of a policy of abundance. At this time also the government increased pensions, health insurance, family allowances, paid holidays and redeployment of the unemployed – to the accompaniment of a continuous rash of strikes.

Political and social order, indeed, were not easily restored. For many months the most explosive issue continued to be the weeding out of collaborators – except for the problem of King Leopold's return, with which the word collaboration had become most unhappily linked. During the war, the Rexist and VNV collaborators with the Gestapo had certainly terrorized their own compatriots in lawless killings unparalleled, according to some Belgians, since the days of the Duke of Alva. Now there was an impassioned settling of scores that inevitably made justice and equity increasingly hard to establish. For instance, factory owners accused of collaboration argued that if they had closed down their unemployed workers would certainly have been deported, and the factory's machinery might well have been dismantled. Within a year over 330,000 people found themselves accused of *incivisme* or bad citizenship, though the mass of the public, as elsewhere in Europe, had been neither collaborators nor resistance workers but had desperately sought their own survival through behaviour that ranged from semi-collaboration and passive submission to necessity, to small acts of defiance of the occupier and, latterly, intermittent partial resistance. No less than 53,000 persons were condemned, among them almost twice as many Flemings as Walloons. Some 250 death sentences were carried out, although many more accused were condemned to death but not executed. In time many of these sentences were mitigated; and from the beginning the Catholic party was milder than the Left on the question of reprisals. Indeed one of the main accusations of the Left – which claimed to have been the backbone of the resistance – was that both the VNV and the Rexists had been specifically Catholic, and that although the Church had repudiated Rexism, it had never condemned the VNV. This encouraged an intense resurgence of antagonism between Flemings and Walloons, which soon led the Walloons to launch a separatist movement. They urged the creation of three autonomous regions: the two linguistic areas, and Brussels. Others accepted the unitary state, probably from the realization that neither linguistic region was economically viable alone; but they proposed a 'geographical' Senate made up of equal numbers of Flemings and Walloons, to offset Flemish numerical preponderance in the Chamber. A small group advocated union with France.

Under the stimulus of post-war democratic feeling the Catholic party, as in most other European countries, aimed at reform along the lines of Christian Democracy. In August 1945 the traditional Catholic party changed its name to *Parti Social Chrétien* (Christian Social Party) in an appeal to post-war socializing trends. The PSC also asked the Catholic hierarchy to refrain from giving directions on political questions from the pulpit, as it had traditionally done. In the first post-war elections of February 1946 the PSC won 92 seats, a gain of 19 since 1939, some of the votes being gained from the VNV and the Rexists, who vanished completely. Despite its leading position in the elections, however, the PSC continued the Catholic boycott of office begun the previous summer because of its disagreement with the Left over the question of King Leopold's return. Eventually Van Acker formed a ministry of Socialists, Liberals and Communists – united in little except hostility to the King – which held only a bare majority until the Catholics returned to office the following spring after the Communists had resigned. Communist withdrawal was touched off by a wrangle over coal subsidies, but was part of a pattern common to other European coalitions. Paul-Henri Spaak now formed a cabinet of Socialists and Catholics of Christian-Democrat leanings, all of the latter youngish and all holding ministries for the first time.

During this ministry there were hopes of enacting more measures reflecting the general leftward swing of public opinion felt through most of Europe, as it had been after the first world war. There were no radical schemes for nationalization, but a series of measures initiating some workers' control as well as some state regulation of the economy. The state also became a shareholder in the National Bank, appointing the senior directors and determining the upper limit of note-issue, as well as assuming some indirect control of the railroad companies.

During these years a shortage of labour for the mines became a great handicap to economic development. Coal production dropped to half its 1939 level; oil and electricity became widely used, and foreign workers, mainly Italians, began to displace refugees and German prisoners at the coal face. In 1947 a census was held, revealing more than a million more Flemish citizens than Walloons. This in turn led to long-delayed changes in the electoral law, increasing the total number in the lower Chamber from 202 to 212, eight of the new seats going to the Flemish areas. Women were henceforward also to be given the vote.

FOREIGN POLICY

After the war Belgium became a founder member of the United Nations, with Paul-Henri Spaak as first president of its General Assembly. The Benelux organization, launched in September 1944, was the fruit of discussions between representatives of the three countries in wartime London, when they had agreed to create conditions leading to complete economic union by establishing a customs union but excluding, for the time being, agriculture. Belgium was also one of the members of the Organization for European Economic Cooperation which grew out of the 1947 Marshall Plan. Paul-Henri Spaak was elected chairman of this new organization when still Prime Minister and Foreign Minister. In March 1948 Belgium was a signatory, together with her Benelux partners and Britain and France, of the Brussels Treaty, to prepare joint action if attacked in Europe. A year later this nucleus grew into the North Atlantic Treaty Organization, when the United States and Canada, together with other European powers, formed a power bloc against the Communist states, each member pledging itself to rearm as well as accepting American protection through the deterrent threat of the atomic bomb. On 5 May of the same year, the Treaty of London set up the Council of Europe which Belgium joined, with Spaak as president of its Consultative Assembly.

THE ROYAL QUESTION

An early indication that there was to be no easy reconciliation between King Leopold and his government had come a few days after Pierlot's return to Belgium in 1944, when he received a document written by Leopold in January of that year in which the King gave his views on the main postwar problems but also categorically refused to work with the exiled leaders unless they made full public apology to him for their accusations at the time of the capitulation. This they refused, and the King in turn found himself in exile, first in Austria and then in Switzerland. After the formation of Van Acker's cabinet in February 1945, Foreign Minister Spaak was the sole survivor from the Pierlot government, but by that time the question of the King's return had become a national, if not a racial, affair. The Catholic Flemings, by the very nature of their traditional political thinking, were predominantly conservative and therefore imbued with respect for Leopold as their 'natural prince'. The Walloons with equal conviction adhered to French freethinking radicalism – with the exception of the Catholics from the thinly-populated areas of rural Luxembourg and Namur. From the start, therefore, Leopold became identified with the more conservative party through its championship of him. On the other hand, only a small minority of extreme left-wing Socialists and Communists advocated a republic, the Socialist rank and file agreeing with Van Acker when he said 'Belgium needs the monarchy as she needs bread' as an essential rallying point for the two linguistic groups.

But that did not make them want Leopold. The Socialists and Communists demanded outright abdication in favour of Leopold's eldest son Prince Baudouin, while the Catholics favoured his un-conditional return. Therefore, when Van Acker passed a bill barring the King's return without parliamentary consent the Catholics with-drew from his coalition. Their non-support hampered the work of reconstruction, but their indignation increased after the Left set out its indictment of Leopold in a big debate begun on 20 June. In it, every action of the unhappy days of May and June 1940 was re-examined. In addition, Leopold was accused of treating with the enemy by visiting Hitler at Berchtesgaden and of leaving his captivity several times to stay with a pro-Nazi aristocrat in Austria. His wartime entourage was also accused of association with leading Belgian collaborators; but more than any other charge the royal marriage touched off popular emotion, not only because of the unconstitutionality of having the religious wedding three months before the civil ceremony but also because, Van Acker contended, the King should be 'the very incarnation of the sufferings endured by his people'.

Some weeks before the general elections of February 1946, King Leopold proposed that they should be followed by a 'national consultation' on the question of his return and that to this end both he and the government should open their respective dossiers to inspection. As the government continued to insist, after the elections, that parliament was the sole legal expression of the will of the people, Leopold of his own accord appointed a nine-man commission of leading Flemish, Walloon and Brussels figures, to examine files that he made available to them. The commission published a long report in March 1947, essentially vindicating the King. At this time the Catholics returned to office in a coalition with the Socialists, and during its two-year lifetime the royal question came no nearer solution, although Spaak had several interviews in Switzerland with the King. In the elections of June 1949 the Catholic party gained thirteen seats and Spaak fell from office; his own wartime career was once more examined and criticized by his Catholic adversaries.

The Liberals, now in a new Catholic-Liberal coalition under Gaston Eyskens, agreed to a consultation on the royal question. However, the Liberals stipulated that at least half the electorate in each linguistic region should vote for Leopold, and that he must obtain a two-thirds majority in the country as a whole. This was an adaptation of the Belgian law on amendments to the constitution; but Leopold rejected it in favour of a majority of 55 per cent. In fact, when the country was called to the polls on 12 March 1950, he won 57.68 per cent of the total vote with an average of 72 per cent in the Flemish areas, 42 per cent in Wallonia and 48 per cent in Brussels. The votes in his favour exceeded those given to the Catholic party in the recent elections. However, the Liberals judged Leopold's overall majority too small. The coalition broke down and during the following month's impasse the Liberals swung over against the King, whereupon Leopold offered to resign temporarily, in favour of Baudouin. This the Left rejected.

The Catholics won three more seats in the elections of the following June and so held their first absolute majority for thirty years – mostly at the expense of the Liberals, who were blamed, among other things, for their vacillation over the royal question. However, the PSC won only 47 per cent of the votes of the entire electorate, as the Socialists complained when a new all-Catholic cabinet was formed under Jean Duvieusart. A two-week joint session of both Chambers was endlessly turbulent, against a background of strikes and demonstrations. On 20 July, 197 Catholics of the united Chambers voted for Leopold's return, during a walk-out by the other parties. Two days later Leopold arrived at Laeken from Switzerland. He broadcast that day, asking his people to unite and forget. On 27 July came the famous scene described earlier in this book, when Spaak led demonstrators to Laeken palace. Within the next few days, half a million Socialists and Communists came out on strike in Wallonia, to cries of 'Hang Leopold' and with banners saying 'Our Queen Astrid did not deserve this'. Trains were immobilized, trams overturned, main roads were strewn with nails, traffic in the port of Antwerp was paralysed. Barricades went up in the streets of Liége; fights broke out between Socialist and Catholic trade unionists. When, at Grace Berleur near Liége, three Socialist demonstrators were killed by the police, 100,000 marchers headed for Brussels and all three main political parties met to agree that abdication was the only way to forestall civil war. Leopold hesitated, suggesting once more a temporary delegation of his powers to Baudouin. But he faced the opposition of most of the Catholics who had voted his return. Early on 1 August, the government announced that King Leopold would be replaced by his eldest son; on 11 August Baudouin swore the oath as the Prince Royal; the following July Leopold's abdication was complete, and Baudouin became King.

The long affair had inflamed passions for years, and left a tragic legacy often compared by Belgians to France's Dreyfus case, where families became bitterly and passionately divided. Ever since, Catholics have reminded Socialists that they, the legal majority, were forced to submit to coercion and to mob violence, while Walloon intransigence was no doubt partly caused by panic awareness that on any issue they could now be permanently outvoted. Although the clash of opinion did not wholly follow the linguistic division within the country, it coincided with it sufficiently to make the cleavage between Flemings and Walloons very deep; tragically, the long-accumulated rancour between the two rival groups became concentrated round the person of the King. Belgium came close to disintegration, and for the first time a monarch was the source of discord instead of being the country's natural arbiter and the keystone of the national arch.

However, the social agitation gradually died down and life returned to normal, except that the Catholic party was deeply shaken within itself, its extreme right wing blaming the ministers for not standing up to the threat of an uprising. The next four years of Catholic government were notable domestically for some controversial schools legislation and an aggravation of the coalmining problem, while in foreign policy, under the ministry of Paul Van Zeeland, Belgium shared in launching the scheme for integrating Europe represented by the Schuman Plan, and later in the abortive European Defence Community.

There was a drop in the Catholic vote at the elections of 1954; another phenomenon was the sharp increase in Socialist gains in Antwerp and other Flemish cities. Certainly, a revival of anti-clericalism was the chief cement leading to a coalition between Socialists and Liberals under Van Acker. It soon showed itself in a series of school laws proposed by Socialist Minister Leo Collard that launched Belgium – fated to turbulence – once more into a school war.

According to statistics published in 1955 when Collard's bill was laid before parliament, there were more Catholic than lay schools at every level – primary, secondary, teachers' training and technical schools. These Catholic schools were then receiving some 2,000 million Belgian francs a year in state subsidies, which for economy reasons the bill proposed to cut by 15 per cent. This still left a generous sum though it reversed increases made by Education Minister Harmel in the previous administration. Catholic anger was particularly aroused, however, by Socialist attacks on the existing secondary education. Communes and provinces being free under Belgian practice to build what schools they thought fit, a haphazard jumble of small, variously-equipped schools had arisen; and Harmel's attempts to rationalize this, said the Socialists, left Catholics in privileged positions so that the theoretical freedom of choice of the parents was valid only for Catholics. There were also enormous disparities in the funds available, in the Socialist view, since nuns and priests of the teaching Orders personally received very little

99

of the state salaries paid to them; consequently this money could be spent on amenities the state schools found it difficult to provide.

Collard pushed through a bill 'equalizing' the situation by allotting grants for more official schools, as well as measures increasing state control of all education. After the bill was signed by King Baudouin, rioting broke out when Collard's effigy was publicly burned or hanged, Catholics no doubt being determined to show the Left that they too could compel a reversal of decisions taken by a legal majority. In this they eventually succeeded after months of social unrest, when a commission of Socialists, Liberals and Catholics together laboriously worked out a complex school pact of 53 articles, which became law in 1959. Broadly, this now gives equal support at all levels to Church and non-Church schools, the two educational networks remaining separate and distinct but being organized and financed along practically identical lines, with equal aid from the state treasury.

The school war had two more general results. First, it evoked great cohesion from all social levels of the Catholic party – which had suffered bitter internal quarrels, partly connected with the aftermath of the royal question. Secondly, it went back on a principle that the PSC had adopted only ten years before, of keeping religious allegiances separate from political action. In the school affair, the Catholic clergy had once more openly taken the lead, through letters read from the pulpit, in exhorting the faithful to political resistance.

Although this long-drawn-out struggle had absorbed a good deal of public attention, there was some domestic concern at signs of unrest in the Congo, now awakening into political awareness and influenced also by the government's move to establish state schools in the colony. During 1958, however, Belgium showed a confident and prosperous face to the world during the Brussels World Fair, which attracted a record number of 41 million visitors. In this same year the organizations of the Common Market and of Euratom were established in Brussels; Belgium with France, West Germany, Italy and her Benelux partners had signed the Rome Treaties in 1957, after months of complex bargaining in Brussels' Val Duchesse château under the chairmanship of indefatigable Paul-Henri Spaak.

The year 1959 was clouded by the gathering storm in the Congo and by increasing economic difficulties at home. Early in 1960 a Round Table conference was held in Brussels between Belgian and Congolese leaders, when independence for the Congo was fixed for only six months later. By July chaos had struck this newest and richest of the independent African states. Partly in reaction to this catastrophe, Gaston Eyskens' Catholic-Liberal government launched a comprehensive austerity programme presented to the country in September 1960. Despite these troubles, King Baudouin's wedding was celebrated on 15 December to a lady of the Spanish nobility, Doña Fabiola de Mora y Aragón, amidst great general rejoicing. Soon after, however, the trade unions rose against the austerity law in a long winter strike that was once more accompanied by a great explosion of public unrest. Ostensibly the Belgian public was little concerned with the Congo débâcle; but the loss of her once-model colony was undoubtedly a blow to Belgium's pride as well as to her pocket. How Belgians came to win and lose this great possession is a study to which we must now turn.

8 The Congo

WITH THE HISTORIAN'S ADVANTAGE of hindsight, one can claim that the Congo story began in London in 1817, when the talented and ambitious Leopold of Saxe-Coburg-Gotha lost his first wife Princess Charlotte, heiress to the British throne. On her death all Leopold's hopes of ruling indirectly over the world's most powerful nation were lost, but throughout his life he retained his dreams of empire, and transmitted them in full to the son who succeeded him. During his long reign as the first Belgian king, Leopold made almost fifty little-known attempts to establish Belgian interests overseas, in places as far apart as Guatemala, Abyssinia and the coasts of Guinea.[1] Partly, it is true, he was in search of trading stations to compensate Belgium for the loss of her openings in the Dutch East Indies; partly he sought new opportunities for the 900,000 paupers who lived on public charity in the 1840s. There is no doubt that he also felt his own talents constricted within the narrow boundaries of his new country.

Leopold II inherited all his father's energy and ambition, and felt even more like a caged eagle. Already in 1860 he had written, 'surrounded by Holland, Prussia and France, our European frontiers can never be extended. Our neutrality forbids us any political activity in Europe. But the sea bathes our coast, the universe lies before us'.[2] As a young man he travelled widely, particularly in the Near and Far East. After one voyage he presented Belgium's leading statesman Frère-Orban with a piece of marble from the Acropolis with the engraved sentence 'Belgium must have a Colony'. But his enthusiasm aroused little response from his compatriots, either then or later. By nature Belgians were deeply attached to their own localities; even the sharp population rise of the nineteenth century inspired little move to leave home for wider spaces. Such exodus as existed was usually towards France or to the United States; but it was never considerable, and in face of this lack of interest for his colonizing schemes Leopold II, like his father, grew quiet and even secretive about them.

Soon after he succeeded to the throne in 1865, Leopold began a number of attempts to acquire land in places such as upper Paraguay, Borneo and the Philippines. In 1875, disappointed at his lack of success, he decided 'to make discreet inquiries as to whether there is not something to be done in Africa'.[3] By then a series of British explorers – Livingstone, Speke and Grant, Baker, and Lovett Cameron – had done immense pioneering work in Central Africa, and Stanley was already in the middle of the 7,000-mile trek which was to lead him from Zanzibar via Lakes Victoria and Tanganyika along the Congo River from one of its sources to its mouth at Boma. No word had been heard of him for some time when in 1876 Leopold decided to call a Geographical Conference in Brussels, with the aim 'of co-ordinating European efforts at exploration and at suppression of the African slave trade'. This sounded an admirably philanthropic venture, and attracted delegates from all the leading European countries, particularly as Leopold, king of a small neutral state which took little interest either in colonization or the conference, seemed a suitable figurehead for any co-ordinated action.

An International African Association was formed, with an executive committee chaired by Leopold in Brussels, but with so few real powers that the Association was virtually stillborn. It met only once more, in June 1877, when its chief business was to design its own flag – blue, with a gold star in the centre. Soon after, Stanley's descent of the Congo to Boma became known in Europe; and Leopold transformed the Association into a *Comité d'Etudes du Haut Congo* composed of businessmen from most of the Association's member countries, to study trade prospects in the Congo basin. Stanley agreed to lead an expedition for the *Comité*. But even before he got back to the Congo in 1879 it had dissolved itself, and Leopold was left alone to provide Stanley with funds and so to take full control of the enterprise. He formed a new *Association Internationale du Congo*, which in spite of its name was merely Leopold's instrument; but he did so discreetly, to avoid arousing international jealousy or the disapproval of his own compatriots.

Ignorant of these niceties and of the air of mystery that surrounded his enterprise, Stanley stayed in Africa for three years, hacking and hewing his way through forest and swamp in fulfilment of his mandate to reach Stanley Pool, 300 miles upriver beyond the cataracts. With him he took a small flotilla (consisting of Leopold's Cowes yacht, the *Royal*, a twin-screw steamer of 30 tons displacement, two steam launches, two lighters, a wooden whaleboat, and a paddle-boat 43 feet long) for use beyond the Pool, together with material for building and quantities of cloth and so on for exchange with the Congolese tribes. To make a road to transport this vast load round the cataracts was a Herculean task, probably impossible without strong-arm tactics. Leopold became uneasy at Stanley's methods, but the latter's justification of his own brutality may have given the King an early conviction that in the Congo squeamishness had no place.[4]

Soon Leopold had other anxieties; in the early 1880s Portugal, which had traded near the Congo mouth for centuries, began to claim the right to control it: even worse, the explorer de Brazza was hastening through Gabon to plant the French flag at Stanley Pool. In the spring of 1882 Stanley reached the opposite shores of the Pool and erected a new station, Leopoldville, three miles away from the French encampment. He thought his task was over; but after a brief respite in Europe he was back in Africa in Leopold's employ, and from Leopoldville travelled 1,200 miles along the Congo to Stanley Falls, exploring, setting up stations, and negotiating concessions with local tribes. When he returned to Europe in 1884 the blue flag of King Leopold's Association was planted in an area vast enough at last to attract the attention of rival European powers.

THE BERLIN CONFERENCE

By this time the scramble for Africa was gathering speed, but the German Chancellor Bismarck was chiefly motivated by considerations of European politics when he called an international conference on Africa in November 1884. For three months discussions ranged over free trade and freedom of navigation in Africa, the protection of the indigenous peoples and the problem of the slave trade. The official agenda did not include the question of territorial rights in the Congo at all; nor was the Association officially present. But Bismarck inquired what the *Association Internationale du Congo* represented, and King Leopold's role in it thus came to light. Great Britain did not want to occupy the Congo basin; trade, and the suppression of the slave trade were her main interests. On the other hand Britain did not intend to let France take possession either. Bismarck did not wish to see either England or France in the Congo; therefore he moved that all the Powers present should follow the lead of the United States and of Germany in recognizing Leopold's Association as the valid government of an independent territory. It was to be neutral like Belgium – although, by the express wish of the Belgian parliament, Belgium itself was to have no link with the new state except the King. Certainly Leopold won this diplomatic triumph because the Powers considered him a petty monarch and therefore harmless. But when he was proclaimed Sovereign of the Congo Free State at Boma in July 1885 he became in fact the absolute ruler of almost a million square miles of African territory, eighty times the size of Belgium. The Saxe-Coburgs had indeed won themselves a place in the sun.

THE CONGO FREE STATE

But, jubilant as he was, Leopold realized that great problems lay before him, not least the problem of finding money to open up his new empire.The Powers had granted him the right to levy export duties; and after an Anti-Slavery Conference held in Brussels in 1889 he was also allowed to impose an import tax of 10 per cent. But before any volume of trade could exist there must be more exploration; more investigation of the land's potential riches was needed, plus some rudimentary forms of administration and policing, without which no effective occupation could exist.

Early explorations had shown that the Congo basin contained an immense network of navigable rivers; they were to become as important to the development of the new territory as the Meuse and the Scheldt had been in Belgium's own early history. But between these great highways and the coast lay the series of cataracts near the river mouth; as Stanley had foreseen, rapid development of the new state could not begin without a railway up to Stanley Pool.

Perpetually short of money, short of credit and short of experienced personnel, Leopold risked the whole of his personal fortune, and ran heavily into debt during the early years. Almost from the start, therefore, he began a system that he later authorized by his own decree, namely to allow his agents (less than half of them Belgian), in the name of the state, to buy from natives ivory and rubber, at prices also fixed by the state. His officials were paid a commission according to the amounts of ivory and rubber they acquired – also necessary to supplement their very meagre pay. All territory not occupied by Africans (in this sparsely-populated land this meant about half the entire area) was considered vacant and reserved to the exclusive use of the state. Africans hunting in these areas were forbidden to sell ivory or rubber to private traders.

There were obvious opportunities for abuse inherent in such a system, where the agents of the law were also traders with a direct interest in the profits to be made. The fact that it arose at all was evidence of Leopold's lack of means. It also showed the primitiveness of his new realm, where a money economy was virtually unknown; he was soon also driven to impose a tax in labour. What his Negro subjects were to receive in return for these unwelcome taxes seemed clear, at least in Europe: they were to be given the blessings of civilization.

To the twentieth-century mind this may sound a doubtful return, but at the time white men everywhere, particularly the confident, aggressive kind attracted to pioneering, were intoxicated by the newness of their own technical discoveries, which inevitably fed their sense of superiority. The steamers, the railroads and the knowledge of medicine that made the penetration of Africa possible widened the gap between black and white cultures. Only rare individuals like David Livingstone or Dan Crawford[5] had the humility to want to learn from Africans as well as to teach them.

King Leopold was neither humble, nor sensitive, nor patient; but he was not altogether without scruples. He forbade the sale of alcohol to natives, he fostered research into tropical medicine; he did his utmost to encourage the growth of Belgian missionary settlements; and he quite skilfully combined the suppression of the slave trade, entrusted to him in Berlin, with the establishment of his own authority.

But the anti-slavery wars, with their Belgian heroes so well-known to every Belgian schoolchild, did not begin until the 1890s. Before that, Leopold established and trained a force of Congolese under Belgian army officers to put down intertribal quarrels and the local revolts that flared up as his titular occupation of the Congo basin was gradually made effective.

Some tribes were more recalcitrant than others, but Leopold left to the missionaries – most of them Protestants from England and America in the earliest days – the task of studying tribal ways and tribal languages. He himself constantly stretched his resources to their limits in his anxiety to make himself real master, and also to keep out potential white rivals. Chief of these was Cecil Rhodes; it is one of the ironies of African history that the Katanga was won for Leopold with the help of British agents. The existence of rich copper deposits there was already known to him. But development did not begin until the early twentieth century, mainly for lack of capital to establish communications.

In 1890 Leopold secured a ten-year loan of 25 million francs from the Belgian State; and in return he promised to bequeath his huge Congo fief to Belgium in his will, an offer that aroused little public enthusiasm. Only after the first locomotives reached Stanley Pool in 1898 did Belgian private capital begin to flow and Belgian suspicions of the vast, doubtful venture begin to wane. Up to 1895 Leopold had been deeply in debt; but by that year the profit on ivory sales began to mount, and his income then rose exceedingly rapidly. According to a Belgian estimate the King's private domain made a clear profit of nearly three million sterling in the ten years from 1896 to 1906.[6] But while he grew rich on his ivory and rubber taxes his black subjects received little civilizing in return. As the money came in he did not change or relax his early system; and when voices began to be raised in criticism, he steadfastly believed that the prime motive was not humanitarianism but jealousy.

The earliest reports of extortions by state agents came from Protestant missionaries; British stories swelled into an international chorus after J. B. Murphy, an American, told Reuter in 1895 that Africans in the Equator area were often shot if they failed to bring in enough rubber. Stories of forced labour, pillage and mutilation led a Liverpool journalist, E. D. Morel, to found the Congo Reform Society, with a wealth of detail on abuses and of facts and figures on profits. The Italian consul in Matadi published a 23-page dossier on atrocities. Public outcry led the British government in 1903 to ask its consul at Boma, Roger Casement, to investigate and report.

The Morel and Casement documents caused an outcry both in Britain and the United States for the Congo Free State to be withdrawn from its absolute monarch and put under Belgian control. In reply, King Leopold sent his own commission of inquiry in 1904 and its report, though mildly worded, bore out the substance of the missionaries' charges. When in the following years a Belgian Jesuit and an anti-Catholic lawyer each advocated, after studying the report, that Belgium must annex the Congo, Belgian public opinion became thoroughly aroused. Many go-ahead firms now favoured annexation because they suffered from King Leopold's monopoly of trade. On the other hand the Socialists disapproved in principle of colonialism, and in any case felt money should be invested at home, to improve the lot of the ill-paid Belgian workers. Leopold felt that the Congo should become Belgian only after his death and bitterly resented his empire being taken from him by men who had shared none of his risks. He failed in his hopes of keeping the Crown Domain for himself, but succeeded in delaying the take-over by fanning resentment against foreign – especially British – criticisms. In August 1908 the parliament voted in favour of annexation, and on 15 November of the same year the Congo Free State ceased to exist, and became the Belgian Congo.

Leopold died in the following year at the age of seventy-four. In his prosperous last years he had launched a long-cherished programme to give Belgium the embellishments he felt his country should have, spending freely out of his own pocket on botanical and zoological gardens, public monuments and museums; his avenues and parks in Brussels transformed the city. In his later years he was none the less thoroughly unpopular. His restless schemes for world-wide investments led his subjects to accuse him of megalomania; but in his cold way he had sincerely wished his nation to share his visions. He was a great man greatly flawed.

THE HAPPY COLONY

Belgium took up her new responsibilities in the Congo without jubilation, but with the determination to rule well. Within a few years the monopoly system was abandoned and private commerce stimulated; the Congolese were encouraged to trade freely, and the tax in labour or in kind was abolished in favour of a money tax. The *Banque du Congo* was founded, with Belgian capital and its own currency. There was a great drive to recruit responsible men as state officials, and to pay them attractive salaries. The Universities of Brussels and of Louvain began courses in colonial studies which, with the University Institute of Antwerp, gradually developed an outstanding body of knowledge on the Congo.

Legislation for the colony, according to the Charter of 1908, was by royal decree, the King exercising his prerogatives through a minister of the Colonies with the advice of a Colonial Council of fourteen nominees, usually men with knowledge of the Congo as administrators, missionaries, lawyers or industrialists. The Belgian parliament controlled but did not initiate legislation; it also approved the budget. However, parliamentary interest died down after the early years, and the minister became the sole effective source of authority, to whom the Governor-General in Leopoldville and the Vice-Governor in Katanga were also responsible.

Education of the twelve million Congolese was entrusted entirely to the Church, and followed a pattern agreed between Leopold and the Vatican in 1906. By this concordat, Roman Catholic missions were given perpetual grants of land and subsidies in exchange for establishing schools to teach government-approved curricula. This system developed very widely, without any major change, until after World War II. The first Congolese was ordained priest in 1917; thirty years later there were over three hundred African priests, and the Congo had one of the highest literacy levels in the continent. Sincere concern for the 'moral elevation' of the Congolese featured in this successful alliance of Church and State; it also had the advantage of spreading education cheaply through the more accessible areas of the Congo's vast and often primitive regions.

A third great power in the colony was that of the big companies. Some of the large-sized firms had received their concessions in Leopold's day and from then onwards increasingly dominated industrial production. Among these were the *Comité Spécial du Katanga*, founded in 1900, which owned freehold rights over some 35 million acres. *Forminière*, created in 1906, was authorized to develop the subsoil over half the Congo, including the diamond mines of Kasai. *Union Minière* controlled a much smaller area but it included the immensely rich copper deposits of Haut Katanga. Among the earliest investors were also the Lambert, Empain, Francqui and Thys groups; some of these, together with *Forminière, Union Minière* and others came under the control of the powerful *Société Générale*. Gradually this great Belgian holding company came to influence some 70 per cent of the total Congolese economy. Mining was and remained the basic source of wealth, but agricultural production developed rapidly during the first world war, when the colony exported valuable raw materials such as rubber and palm oil as well as copper, gold and tin.

As the tightly linked networks of companies grew in size and number, their power became dominant in the areas they controlled. Needing to build up a reliable labour force from the Congo's sparse population, they had every incentive to collaborate with the government and the missions in establishing for their workers decent levels of education, housing, medical services and law and order. Development was checked during the recession of the 1930s; but trade revived and output began to include cobalt, zinc, manganese and lead, with hydroelectric power as a new source of energy. Visitors who remembered the early days found the changes astonishing.

Visitors were welcome, but otherwise the Congo was virtually insulated from the outside world. Belgium did not encourage white immigration; the authorities – and the home-loving Belgians they recruited – preferred trained men to spend fifteen or twenty years in the Congo under contract, but not to settle. While they were in the colony they lost their voting rights at home; no kind of colonial parliament was envisaged, and any form of voting remained unknown to the Congolese.

All authority flowed out to the Congo from Brussels. Centralization and paternalism were practised by all three of the omnipotent trinity: Church, State and companies. If the white men on the job were excluded from policy-making, even less did it occur to anyone to prepare the Congolese to share it. And at that time the Congolese themselves showed no such ambitions; even the traditional authority of their local chiefs was eroded gradually as Belgian control spread. From time to time there were rebellions against white power, most notably the Kimbanguist and Kitawala religious movements. But on the whole the Congolese were well satisfied to receive health, security, instruction and an improved standard of living from their Belgian rulers. So the system continued until World War II, admired by all who knew it, a source to Belgium both of wealth and satisfaction.

INDEPENDENCE

From World War II onwards industrial production in the Congo increased at a phenomenal rate; the value of its exports rose from $45 million in 1938 to $540 million in 1956. By 1956 a quarter of the 13 million population was living in towns, and in these urban areas the pattern of benevolent paternalism was rapidly intensified. Family allowances, sickness and old-age pensions followed the wide extension of other social provisions such as maternity clinics, social centres, and sports grounds, in addition to the increasing network of churches, schools and hospitals. There was a parallel increase in the numbers of Congolese trained as clerks, mechanics, medical assistants and so on until a distinct middle class developed, well paid by African standards but with a wide gap between their wages and those of the lowest-paid whites. In 1947 the Catholic University of Louvain created a university centre, named Lovanium, as a first step towards the organization of higher education; but university degrees for Congolese were considered out of the question. 'No élites, no trouble' was the slogan.

But the Congo had been shaken by the war years. For the first time some Congolese had seen something of the world, when troops served in Egypt and in the Middle East. They became aware of developments elsewhere, especially of the moves towards independence of other African territories. At home there were also changes; the whites, cut off from Belgium for four years, resented the restoration of the tight control of Brussels. During the war they had gone on strike, and had established trade unions, both being practices previously frowned on. From 1946 they even raised ideas of home rule for the Congo on the lines of the British dominions. This wish was strongest in Katanga, which had close contacts with the Rhodesias and with South Africa. Katanga had also long favoured decentralization, complaining that her rich province was the milch cow both for Leopoldville and for Brussels.

All the various demands of the whites were made for themselves, not for the Congolese. But the latter were quick to add their own claims. In 1946 they secured a voice on works councils and in the following year began to represent native interest on state councils. More and more they complained of the inequalities of pay, of segregation in housing, in the schools and in social life, of the government's strict censorship of news, and its severity with its critics. Reluctantly, the authorities gave way inch by inch.

Soon the Congolese also learned to play off Belgian domestic quarrels to their own advantage, especially the perennial rivalry between Flemings and Walloons. In 1958, although the companies employed a majority of Walloons, 53 per cent of the administrators and 83 per cent of the missionaries were Flemish; Flemings had done much in the schools to keep the four vernacular languages of the Congo as the main languages of instruction, out of a mixture of respect for mother tongues and from a dislike of *fransquillon* Congolese. But as the Africans evolved they began to feel that this was a deliberate attempt to hold back their intellectual development; they particularly objected to the compulsory study of Flemish in the post-war secondary schools. These resentments came to be coupled with an increasing dislike of the authoritarianism of the Roman Catholic Church. (Many Congolese believed that Catholicism was the religion of 'little Belgium' while powerful nations like Great Britain and the United States were Protestant.) But the Church's strong hold over education meant there was no escape, until the 1954 Liberal-Socialist coalition in Belgium appointed an anti-clerical Colonial Minister, Auguste Buisseret, with the avowed aim of breaking the Catholic educational monopoly. A government survey of education in the Congo amounted to a manifesto in favour of secular instruction. As a result, new lay schools were built – teaching exclusively in French – and in 1956 a lay university was founded at Elisabethville, to balance Leopoldville's Lovanium, which for the first time in 1954 began to prepare Congolese students for university degrees.

Another turning-point in these years was a 'Thirty-year plan for the political emancipation of Belgian Africa' published in 1956 by A. A. J. Van Bilsen, a Belgian with a wide knowledge of African affairs both within and outside the Congo. He deplored Belgium's piecemeal and reluctant changes and proposed a gradual preparation of the Congolese for responsible self-government. His plan was taken up by a Congolese journal, the *Conscience Africaine*. Very soon a more radical organization named the Abako[7] replied in print, rejecting the Van Bilsen plan and demanding self-government forthwith. African excitement and impatience began to mount, and was increased in the same year when France decreed a large measure of autonomy for her colonies. In 1957 Ghana became independent. The Brussels Exhibition of 1958 led Congolese from all over their vast country to meet, and to mix in Brussels with Belgians who taught them much about their own political rivalries; the Socialists in particular impressed the Africans with their hatred of the powerful trust companies. In August, General de Gaulle visited Brazzaville and announced to the French colonies that 'whoever desires independence can immediately obtain it'. Only two days later, the Congolese sent their Governor-General a petition demanding a date for complete independence.

At this time the *Mouvement National Congolais* was founded, and soon became the only political party that found support in all areas of the Congo. It was led by Patrice Lumumba of Stanleyville, then thirty-three years old; in December 1958 he attended the All-African People's Conference held in Accra, and returned home to make fiery speeches full of urgency and unrest. Early in January 1959 rioting broke out in Leopoldville, and for two days Africans wrecked and looted churches, schools and hospitals and attacked Europeans. The whites panicked, called in the army, and at least a hundred people were killed.

Belgians who had continued to believe that all was well in the Congo never recovered from the shock and horror of this outbreak. On 13 January, King Baudouin broadcast, stating that Belgium's aim was to lead the Congolese towards independence 'without procrastination but without undue haste'. Elections by universal suffrage were to be held in the same year, from which an embryo parliament would emerge. An enormous proliferation of political parties and of electioneering followed, in which bewildered Africans came to believe that 'dipenda' would bring the absence of all constraints.[8] They began to refuse to pay taxes. Rioting and tribal fighting broke out. Throughout the year there was a massive flight of European capital. In desperation, the Belgian authorities proposed a Round Table conference in Brussels, held in January and February of 1960.

It was attended by thirteen leading Congolese parties, and the three main Belgian political parties. The Congolese unanimously demanded a date for independence before they consented to consider any other matter. This was fixed for 30 June of the same year, and an enormously complicated *loi fondamentale* with 259 articles modelled on the Belgian constitution was hastily thrown together, to serve pending the creation of a constituent assembly through general elections. These were held in May; after them Patrice Lumumba was declared future prime minister, and the Abako leader, Joseph Kasavubu, future president.

On 30 June King Baudouin attended the independence ceremonies at Leopoldville. On 4 July the Congolese army in Thysville and Leopoldville rebelled against its white officers. Belgians from all over the Congo flew home to Brussels as stories of rape and looting spread. The tragedy of the independent Congo had begun.

Belgium has been greatly blamed for pulling out so abruptly. But given the extent of civil disobedience after the Leopoldville riots, it is impossible to see how Belgian control could have continued except by armed force, and that would have been as unacceptable to Belgium as to the rest of world opinion. In the circumstances there was no 'right' solution. If after independence Belgians had been less panicky and the Congolese less immature, a phased withdrawal of Belgian power might have been achieved to everybody's advantage; but the Belgians on the spot had lost confidence in the Brussels government and deeply distrusted the Congolese. Fearing catastrophe, they helped to precipitate it; in turn the Congolese leaders shirked the responsibilities for which they had clamoured and for which they were so unprepared, absorbing themselves in recriminations and factional rivalries.

POST-INDEPENDENCE

When independence began there were some 80,000 Belgian technicians and administrators in the Congo who were, it was agreed, to remain at their jobs until a Congolese élite was trained to take over; there were also about 20,000 settlers. Virtually all these people had their wives and children with them. These were the Belgians who fled after the Congolese forces mutinied. To protect those who remained, as well as Belgian economic interests, Belgian paratroops were flown in. At this, Patrice Lumumba's government broke off diplomatic relations with Belgium and appealed for help to the United Nations; UN troops went in to restore order – no easy task, since tribal war and pillage spread rapidly after the breakdown of effective government. Katanga, traditionally resentful of control from Leopoldville, proclaimed its independence on 11 July. It soon became the only area that avoided chaos; production (particularly of copper and cobalt ore) continued normally there and Belgian personnel remained at virtually full strength. Belgium was quickly accused

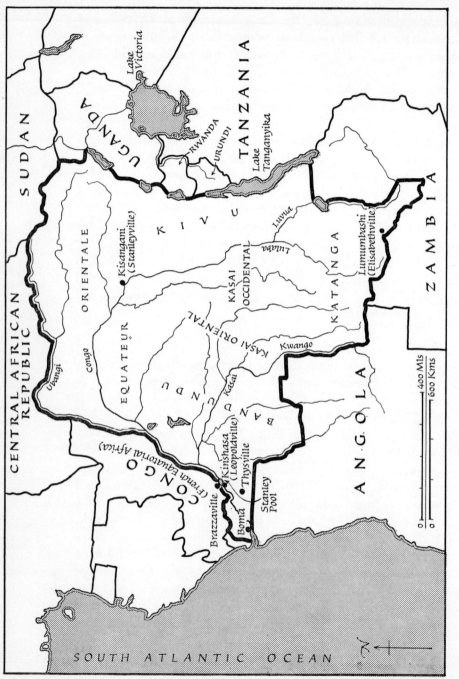

The Democratic Republic of the Congo

of supporting the Katangese secession. When Belgians began to return to the rest of the Congo less than three months after their flight home, they were often at loggerheads with UN officials and Belgium was repeatedly censured in the Security Council. After the death of Patrice Lumumba in February 1961, mobs in Moscow, Belgrade, Cairo and elsewhere led demonstrations accusing Belgium of collusion. At this time there was world-wide condemnation of Belgium's colonization of the Congo, with almost total disregard of the benefits Belgium had undoubtedly brought to her colony through high standards of health, literacy and material wellbeing.

The Belgian government fell, and elections led to the formation of a Catholic-Socialist coalition in May 1961. Foreign Minister Spaak tried to mend Belgium's relations with the United Nations (he had been first President of its Assembly), although feelings were severely strained by the UN troops' attack on Elisabethville in December of that year. During the same month Spaak restored diplomatic relations with the central government, now led by Mr Adoula, and reaffirmed that Belgium would not recognize Katanga's claim to independence.

After another attack by UN troops the Katangese secession ended in January 1963, and this seemed to prepare the way for a settlement of outstanding disputes between the Congolese government and Belgium, especially as by that time the Congolese had invited back nearly 3,000 Belgian technicians, mostly teachers, medical, veterinary and agricultural experts and public administrators. So far in its brief life the Congo republic had known only intense confusion. The United Nations Organization, Americans, Ghanaians, Russians and Chinese had all become involved, and the Congolese now appeared to feel that of all their would-be saviours the Belgians might be the least objectionable. Only they knew the country and its people. About 50,000 company workers were also back in the Congo by this time; most of the Belgian missionaries had never left.

Between 1963 and 1964 the Adoula government worked out a financial agreement with Brussels to decide how many millions of francs each owed to the other, though the maze of complexities was so great that, the Congolese said, 'a cow couldn't find her own calf in it'. However, all this was rejected by Mr Tshombe when he replaced Mr Adoula in mid-1964. By February 1965 Spaak and Tshombe had worked out a new agreement in Brussels. According to this, the independent Congo at last took over shares in the huge holding companies that previously had provided the colony with most of its revenues. These shares were to have been handed over in 1960, but in the unstable situation the Belgian government had held on to them. Belgium had continued, however, to service the Congolese national debt and Congo bonds issued abroad, and was paying out other large sums that technically were the responsibility of the independent Congo, including compensation to Belgian nationals for losses suffered during and after 1960, as well as some $500 million a year for maintaining the returned technicians. Belgium was also educating more than 1,500 Congolese students and trainees in Belgium. When Tshombe left Brussels after the negotiations he took with him a large cheque and a porfolio making the Congolese government a major stockholder in various mining (especially gold-mining), electricity, transport and agricultural companies. Henceforward the Congolese republic would take charge of its own national debt. Brussels agreed in principle to continue and increase her technical aid programme.

Before this agreement came into effect it was once more called into question, after General Mobutu seized power in a bloodless coup on 25 November 1965. Soon after that event, the Union Minière chairman had announced to the company's general assembly that for the first time in four years the annual report had nothing to say of losses, tragic events, military operations or destructions in Haut Katanga; but trouble was not long in coming after President Mobutu – pushed by the youthful extremists who surrounded him – adopted the type of left-wing African nationalism which recognized Patrice Lumumba as its martyred leader. General Mobutu renamed cities, Leopoldville becoming Kinshasa, Elisabethville Lumumbashi, Stanleyville Kisangani, and revived anti-Belgian propaganda. He denounced Tshombe as the tool of the big companies, and claimed that the Spaak–Tshombe agreement would lead to the 'subordination and despoliation' of the Congo. By the Bakajika law passed in the spring of 1966, President Mobutu decreed that the soil and subsoil of the Congo were exclusively Congolese property and that all existing mining concessions were therefore invalid unless they were renewed. He required all companies to register in the Congo, to maintain their headquarters there and to put all their assets under Congolese jurisdiction by the end of 1966.

However, most of the big firms arranged compromises whereby, broadly, the production side of their activities were to be incorporated in the Congo while the sales side would continue to be run from Brussels. This was the solution also worked out between the Congolese government and the Union Minière, by far the most important foreign company since by that time it was providing nearly half the Congolese government's total tax receipts. Suddenly in December 1966 Mobutu unilaterally repudiated this project and proposed conditions which, according to Union Minière, amounted to the transfer to the Congo of virtually all the assets of the company while leaving all the liabilities to the Belgian end.

Relations between the two had always been uneasy and now became openly hostile. The Union Minière refused to move to the Congo, counting on their size and indispensability to deter President Mobutu from carrying out his threatened 'congolization'. However, Mobutu immediately stopped all export of ores and created a new company, the Société Générale Congolaise des Minerais, which on 1 January 1967 took over all the Union Minière assets on Congolese territory including plant and equipment, stocks of products and bank accounts, without compensation. The Congolese government also demanded that the Union Minière should pay some $150 million by mid-January as the estimated value of Union Minière stocks outside the Congo. Otherwise the Congolese republic threatened to take over assets in the Congo belonging to the great Belgian parent company, the Société Générale de Belgique, of equivalent value. The Union Minière rejected this, and in its turn threatened to boycott sales of the products of the new Congolese company, even to suing potential buyers anywhere in the world if necessary.

Meanwhile the Belgian government intervened, protesting against this uncompensated nationalization but offering to mediate between

Belgian industry and the Congolese government; its efforts were soon checked when the Congolese government decided that no foreign technicians could leave the country without giving a year's notice. As the Belgians pointed out, this was legally quite unjustifiable, as Belgian technicians had made no contractual obligation whatsoever with the Congolese government or with the new Congolese company. In any case, all but five of the 1,650 technicians chose to leave the country and eventually the government ceased to try to enforce any conditions on them, and indeed tried to encourage them to remain in the Congo, given their key role and the lack of recruits to replace them.

If the Congolese did not carry out their threats against the technicians, they were on the other hand quick to seize property in payment of part of the $150 million in question, not from the Société Générale de Belgique but from smaller firms that were subsidiaries of the Union Minière in the Congo. This action naturally caused an outcry in Belgium, but at the height of the crisis the Congolese government appointed Mr Theodore Sorensen, a New York lawyer and a former adviser to President Kennedy, to defend its interests in the conflict. At his first meeting with Union Minière representatives in Brussels early in February, Mr Sorensen informed them that the Congolese government had agreed in principle that compensation should be paid for its nationalization of foreign property.

Subsequently the lawyers set up committees of experts to assess the mutual claims of the two sides. By this time the Congolese government was in great need of foreign exchange, all production and therefore all revenues having stopped before the end of December. It still refused to have any new dealings with the Union Minière but, with the latter's acquiescence, agreed to appoint as its sales agent the Société Générale des Minerais – a Belgian firm which, like Union Minière, was a subsidiary of the great Société Générale de Belgique. Its name, confusingly, was almost identical with that of the new Congolese firm – which, however, became known as Gecomin. From 15 February 1967 the Belgian firm (known as SGM) took over the industrial and sales marketing operations for Gecomin, as well as the recruitment and control of non-African personnel. This agreement is to continue for a minimum duration of five years, and thereafter may be abandoned by either side, with two years' notice. The legal wrangle between the claims of the Congolese Republic and of Union Minière continued throughout most of 1967. It would scarcely be true to say that the new arrangements worked with perfect smoothness, but the upshot was that the valuable copper, cobalt, zinc, cadmium and germanium ores continued to be mined and exported, and the Congolese government revenues were assured.

BELGIAN GOVERNMENT AID

On 31 August 1963 a convention had been signed between the Belgian and Congolese governments, according to which over 2,000 technicians, mostly teachers, were to be sent to the Congo and over 1,000 Congolese were to be given technical or university training in Belgium. Similarly, some 500 Belgian specialists were to aid the modernization of the Congolese army. These official agreements replaced the *de facto* co-operation that had continued between the two countries, to varying extents, ever since independence. But virulent attacks by the Congolese radio and Press made life uncomfortable for these Belgians as well as those – some 40,000 – who worked for the companies or for themselves, usually in the cities of the Congolese republic. They were subjected to frequent victimization and sometimes worse. During the summer of 1967 refugees returned home to Belgium, as in 1960, with stories of atrocities; in August the Belgian embassy in Kinshasa was burned down, and voices at home were raised louder than ever, insisting that Belgians should leave the Congo completely and stop the aid from the Belgian treasury, then valued at about $50 million a year.

Despite their material interests, great knowledge and sense of moral responsibility for the Congo, Belgians felt they were cast in the role of permanent scapegoats for Congolese internal difficulties. In turn the Congolese complained that the real villain was the influence of foreign capitalism, particularly the Belgian Société

Générale, which was so powerful that although it remained in the background of disputes it constituted a state within a state, limiting Congolese freedom. However, both the United Nations and the United States were reluctant to see any further Belgian withdrawal. Both were apprehensive of the threat of chaos in the Congo, but funds were not available for increases in United Nations' help.

In July 1967 Belgian and French mercenary forces serving in the Congolese army in Orientale and Kivu provinces rebelled, and the rising was not quelled until November of the same year. The Belgian government was considered partially at fault for failing to take military action against its own citizens (the mercenaries). As a result the Congolese government imposed severe control against all foreigners, which unleashed a wave of looting and killing. Between July and September 1967 almost half of the 40,000 Belgians fled the country. United States aircraft arrived in Kisangani province to help loyal government troops; and the United States ambassador had the prickly and thankless task of acting at key moments as mediator between the Congolese president and his many critics.

As 1967 ended relations between the Congo and Belgium were at their lowest ebb. But at this point the Congolese authorities began to realize that they had over-reacted against the Belgian residents, whose chief interests concerned the safeguarding of Belgian investments and of their own high salaries. The non-return of teachers showed the Congolese how dependent they were on foreign technical assistance, especially from Belgium. The pendulum then began to swing the other way and by the spring of 1968 Belgian technicians began to return in large numbers, and business confidence to be restored. In 1969 the settlement of the Union Minière's claims for compensation, through a new fifteen-year contract, cleared the way for bigger investments. Prince Albert of Liége led a highly successful economic mission to the Congo, General Mobutu paid an official visit to Belgium in November, and by the end of the year the love-hate relationship between the two countries appeared to have mellowed into a series of mutually satisfactory working arrangements, summed up in the treaty of friendship King Baudouin signed in Kinshasa on 30 June 1970.

During the 1960s Belgium began a new policy of spreading her development aid beyond the Congo, so that by 1967 about 3,000 Belgian technicians working in Asia, North Africa and Latin America were supported by their home government. A separate aid arrangement was agreed between Belgium and the ex-trusteeship territories of Rwanda and Urundi, which each attained sovereign status in July 1962.[9]

9   Flemings, Walloons and other worries

THE BIG STRIKE that disrupted Belgium during the winter of 1960–61 ended in stalemate within six weeks, but ten years later the country is still grappling with the profound economic problems that provoked it. There can be no easy or quick solutions to Belgium's basic troubles and despite some remarkable economic changes that have taken place in recent years in the Flemish areas of the country, Premier Gaston Eyskens's austerity aims in 1970 closely resemble those he had preached during his previous term of office a decade earlier.

For the fact is that Belgium, like Britain, lived above her income for many years and has naturally been unwilling to face the moment of truth. Basically the difficulties of the two countries are closely similar: each industrialized early in the last century and each is now saddled with old-fashioned industries and capital equipment that slow them down in the face of modern foreign competition. Moreover, Belgian installations suffered very little damage during World War II, so that the country was able to bask for many years in the afterglow of her post-war prosperity, when her heavy goods enjoyed a seller's market while her rivals re-equipped their own traditional industries with ultra-modern plant and also launched into the new technological age. As in Britain, Belgium's 'old' industries are coal, steel, textiles, electricity-generating and railroad equipment. Some of these, as well as agriculture, have to be maintained by annual subsidies. By 1969 coal production alone had cost Belgium 110 million francs – money that might have been spent more creatively.

Until the Congo won its independence the true state of Belgium's finances was masked, or minimized, by the backing of the Congolese gold reserve. Soon after this was lost, the Common Market boom slowed down and Belgium was forced to fight hard to maintain her high living standards and high rate of employment – as well as facing the challenge of investing for the future. In 1966 the country developed a policy first devised in 1959 to attract foreign capital for launching new industries in the northern, underdeveloped areas and to offer alternative employment to workers in dying industries of the south such as the coal-mines. There has also been considerable effort to modernize existing big enterprises and to create a new infrastructure including autoroutes and waterways.

Many of the mines of the Walloon area have been uneconomic since the 1930s. Only a few of the 150 or so have an economic future; in the smaller and newer Flemish mining district of the Campine some of the pits are now also worked out. The European Coal and Steel Community has been concerned to clear up both the economic and the social problems of mining in Belgium ever since the organization was created in 1952. It has paid more than $120 million out of its common funds to help cure Belgium's ills; but the country hesitated over closing mines until the 1960s because, once closed, a coal-mine is prohibitively expensive to reopen. In the meantime, Belgian coal production had become the most costly in Europe; this in turn increased the production costs of steel and metalworking, chemicals, gas and electricity, as most of these depended largely on coal.

The national Act of 1966 was subsequently approved by the Common Market and by the Coal and Steel Community, and has offered considerable investment incentives for the declining areas of the coal-mines. However, government hopes of attracting foreign capital for new industries such as electronics and chemicals, and of retraining miners for new skilled jobs, have met some setbacks – particularly as the miners, like other European workers, are reluctant to move elsewhere. American investors in particular have been unattracted by the appearance of the area, with abandoned mines, slagheaps, smoke-encrusted buildings and general lack of facilities.[1]

Steel is another of Belgium's basic traditional industries. For centuries the Liége and Charleroi districts have refined iron ore and now produce about 9½ million tons of crude steel a year. This industry also suffers from old-fashioned installations, though efforts have been made to modernize. Another handicap is its location. Europe now prefers coastal sites for the steel industry, as at Genoa, Dunkirk, Ijmuiden and Bremen. Belgium has also launched similar schemes, at Genk near Antwerp and at Zelzaete near Ghent, where a big integrated steel plant is being built,[2] which are resented by Walloons as additional threats to their livelihood.

Since the government first launched its economic expansion programme in 1959 there has been considerable other investment in Flanders. A good part of the new capital has been foreign, mainly American, German and Dutch, and the firms have settled well except that some of them dislike a 1962 law imposing Flemish as the main administrative language. But on the whole they find the Flemings skilled and hardworking; labour is more readily available than in the Walloon areas and rightly or wrongly it is believed to be less strike-prone. Certain towns have also copied the example of Mechelen (Malines) and use their local autonomy to offer cheap land and gas, water and electricity for new factories. Consequently there have been very rapid changes in the once-rural areas of Flanders as modern, clean industries such as electronics and pharmaceuticals have sprung up. Particularly striking is the development of chemicals and petrochemicals around the port of Antwerp, which has also developed large-scale oil refineries and processing plants for metals which now arrive again from the independent Congo, such as copper and tin, uranium and radium, as well as cobalt, essential to jet aircraft. Antwerp also continues to specialize in the cutting of industrial and other diamonds.

There is fierce competition between Antwerp and Dutch Rotterdam, and also with Antwerp's own Flemish neighbours Ghent and Zeebrugge for the port trade. But an air of fresh, thriving prosperity exists in great areas of the north, which makes a striking contrast to the worst of the Walloon south. Flemish patriots claim that their Walloon critics overstress this. They point out that until around 1950 there had constantly been greater unemployment in the Flemish areas. Agriculture, the main occupation, set a generally low level of wages so that education, housing and general living standards were all less advanced than in the south. Consequently, if Walloon progress is now slowing down while in Flanders it is speeding up, the Flemish region still has a great deal of leeway to make up.

The Walloon areas, as we have seen, have not the same attractions to offer. Manpower will not be lacking as the coal-mines continue to close; but the Walloon birthrate is the world's lowest, with an average of only one child per family, in contrast to the four children of most Flemish families except those in the biggest cities. The low Walloon birthrate means fewer young workers in the future. There is no new source of industrial power, and improved communications are needed even more urgently in the Walloon area than in Flanders because of the south's greater distance from the sea. Their side of the picture is by no means all dark; there are still the steel plants, the heavy machinery, the inherent skill of the workers, and much more. But there is also no doubt that the Walloons feel themselves neglected by Brussels governments, now in pursuit of Flemish votes. Even bleaker is the prospect of being a permanent minority in the present unitary state. The Walloon provinces have a population of just over 3 million; bilingual Brussels has about $1\frac{1}{2}$ million, whereas the north now has over $5\frac{1}{2}$ million Flemings.

THE LANGUAGE QUESTION

It is against this economic and social background that the present language problem must be viewed. The Flemish-Walloon dispute has run like filigree throughout the texture of Belgian life for many years, but it now seems that the filigree may have changed into the twisted smouldering fuse of a time bomb, that threatens to split the country apart. Emotions come into play as well as economic facts, and it seems true that one of the strongest underlying feelings is class resentment. Flemings remember that for many years they have been made to feel second-class citizens in their own country. They are determined to break up a social pattern that has been all too common in the past: where in any Brussels or Flemish business office the porter at the door spoke Flemish, the girl secretary was bilingual and the boss knew only French.

The generation that has grown up since the 1932 settlement is most determined to change all this. All who have had a purely Flemish education find that they still need a second language if they are to make their way in the wider world. Yet they have less opportunity to become fluent in French, coupled with a deep unwillingness to feel themselves impoverished without it. Naturally, therefore, they seek to impose themselves within Belgium and being numerically superior, are increasingly doing so in all fields of national life.

For instance, they are now very numerous in the national administration. In their eyes this new phenomenon is merely the overdue correction of an uneven balance. The Walloons and French-speaking Bruxellois, now on the defensive, complain that the bilingualism now required not only for the central civil service but in the business world and many related fields favours the Flemings. The latter have far more incentive to learn French than Walloons have to learn Flemish, a tongue understood only by about 20 million people in the world – mainly Dutch, Flemings and Afrikaners. In protest, many French speakers have their children taught English as a first foreign language.

The linguistic boundary drawn up in 1932 inconveniently does not coincide with boundaries of the provinces. Moreover the law allowed the frontier to change with shifts of population. In 1962 and 1963 the government, under Flemish pressure, passed new laws permanently fixing the frontiers. This led Arthur Gilson, then Minister of the Interior, to remove some villages around Fourons in east Belgium, with 5,000 inhabitants, to the Flemish zone, and a correspondingly small area (with, however, 50,000 people) at Mouscron from West Flanders to French-speaking Hainaut. The latter caused little trouble, but the Fourons transfer led to many months of passionate protest. A bad omen indeed for the greater task of stabilizing the frontier around Brussels.

THE CAPITAL

Brussels has inevitably become an apple of discord coveted by both sides. Historically a Flemish city, its population is now approximately 80 per cent French-speaking. The arrival of the Common

Market and NATO organizations with their influx of diplomats and foreign businessmen has further increased the prevalence of the French language. Yet Brussels lies in the heart of Flemish Brabant, and like every big city is now spilling out rapidly to the surrounding villages. According to the 1932 laws, centres with 30 per cent of population speaking the other language were obliged to provide 'facilities' – for example, a French-speaking postal clerk or policeman, and above all a French-language school. Flemings quite rightly feared that in time the Flemish nature of such villages would be swamped and even extinguished. By the 1962–63 legislation they believed they had achieved recognition of the permanently Flemish character of the six chief disputed communes, or boroughs, limiting French-speaking inhabitants for all time to fewer rights than were allowed in 1932 and certainly excluding French-language schools. The newcomers bitterly resent being condemned to permanent minority status; they argue that local farmers sold 'Flemish soil' at good prices as building plots, and that the new inhabitants should have the right to live as they wish – above all to have their children taught in French at local schools. Flemings for their part are adamant on the school question, believing they are right to give a matter of principle precedence over some admitted hardship. They are particularly vigilant against Flemish families who would themselves like to send their children to French-speaking schools. In the eyes of many Flemings these families are traitors to their own culture, and the French-language schools are 'caste' establishments, producing an élite. All parents who want French-language education for their offspring must pay for them to attend schools in more distant, French-speaking communes.

The 1962–63 laws authorized children in French-speaking schools to be questioned about the language used at home; if it is Flemish, they must transfer to a Flemish school. This overriding of parental rights of decision has always been bitterly contested. In other ways also, life between Flemish and French speakers can become an endless exchange of small slights that makes for much discord. And as commuters pour in from all quarters of tiny Belgium to their daily work, they are caught up willy nilly, by the language they speak, into the city's hostilities and tensions. So the government's hopes have been disappointed that a settlement of the Brussels question would set the scene for a pacification scheme embracing the entire country. On the contrary, the Brussels problem refuses to die.

CONSTITUTIONAL REFORM

From the time of the 1961–65 Christian-Social–Socialist coalition between Lefèvre and Spaak, domestic politics have been dominated by the language question. After passing the 1962–63 laws the Lefèvre coalition began an all-party study of projects for constitutional reform. During the short life of the Harmel–Spinoy Catholic–Socialist coalition that followed, the government tried to carry out some of the previous coalition's recommendations but got no further than putting into effect a long overdue redistribution of parliamentary seats.

The population increase in the Flemish area had caused about half a million Flemings to be under-represented. Some Flemish deputies had 50,000 or more constituents, although the nominal limit was 40,000; on the other hand some Walloon representatives were elected by fewer than 30,000 voters. In April 1965 a law was passed re-allocating some of the 212 seats of the Belgian Lower House so as to give the Flemings their true voting weight. But as they outnumber Walloons in the country by about $2\frac{1}{2}$ millions, the latter have asked for constitutional safeguards against being a permanent minority. This demand is resisted by Flemings, who claim that as they outnumber the Walloons, it is only democratic justice that they should outvote them.

For the time being the problem of guarantees for minorities waits on a solution to the entire constitutional question. When Mr Vanden Boeynants led a new Socialist–Liberal coalition in March 1966, he asked for a two-year truce on the language question so that pressing economic problems could be attended to. But he did not get the truce. From the start his government was troubled, not only over continuing quarrels in Brussels but by violence in the bilingual University of Louvain. As these disturbances finally caused the downfall of the Vanden Boeynants–De Clerq government in February

1968 and also led to the exodus of French-speaking students from Louvain, they deserve closer examination.

LOUVAIN

Louvain, one of Europe's most famous universities, used Latin as its language of instruction for centuries after its foundation in 1425. Throughout the nineteenth century, however, teaching was in French. The fact that the university lies in the Flemish area about ten miles north of the language division caused no particular friction until the language laws of 1932, when Flemish was given equal rights with French in university teaching. Both sections grew fast, so that today, each has about 12,000 students – many of the French speakers being foreigners from all parts of the Catholic world. As a special concession, French-language teachers were allowed schools within the town of Louvain for their children, a privilege that was fiercely contested in 1963 on the grounds that they produced an alien élite in the heart of Flemish Flanders; also that some Flemish parents betrayed their co-linguists by enrolling their own children in these 'caste schools'.

In addition, French-language teachers complained that their section was slowly being starved of the resources necessary to its rapid development; but they made their claims in a high-handed way that was considered offensive to Flemings, and touched off local determination to turn French speakers out altogether to the other side of the language frontier. This, the Flemish patriots said, would 'purify the soil of Mother Flanders'.

Since then riots, students' strikes and fights with the townspeople kept Louvain almost continuously in the Belgian news for years – and also touched off counter-riots and other troubles around Brussels University. There was heavy Flemish pressure on the Belgian bishops, who govern the University (though the state provides 90 per cent of its funds); but in May 1966 they decreed that Louvain should remain bilingual. However, the sporadic outbreaks of trouble continued and seriously disrupted studies. As one despairing professor said, 'You can't get on with serious work if you can only do it with a gendarme in the classroom.' In March 1968 (after a further dispute over extensions to French-language buildings), the Bishop of Bruges, Monsignor de Smedt, broke ranks when he said the French speakers should go. Eight Flemish ministers left the government in sympathy, and the Vanden Boeynants coalition fell. It was followed by 132 days of crisis before M. Gaston Eyskens set up a new Christian-Social–Socialist coalition with two education ministers, two ministers of culture, two ministers for relations between the linguistic communities and an economic counsellor each for Flanders, Wallonia and Brussels.

In the election campaign both Catholics and Socialists split into their Flemish and Walloon wings, running virtually separate campaigns. Only the Party of Liberty and Progress stood out for unity on the plea that neither of the two halves of Belgium is viable alone and that prosperity should come before the language question. They hoped for a landslide, but lost one seat. Both the main parties, on the other hand, lost seats to the small extremist groups, notably the Volksunie and the Rassemblement Wallon, who openly crusade for federalism. The latter made common cause with the Brussels French-language splinter group, the Front Démocratique des Francophones.

Inevitably, the government supported the proposed departure of the Flemish section of Louvain, and new buildings are already planned at Ottignies, about twelve miles away. The transfer is to be spread over ten years; the cost will be borne by the state and is expected to be heavy. This, however, has not brought peace to Louvain. Clergy and lay people alike have been dismayed at the emergence of a left-wing Flemish student group with the slogan 'Against Church and Capital'. At present, the protesters say, only 8 per cent of all workers' children in Belgium get to university; but 25 per cent of the Flemish intake into Louvain is of working-class origin, while among French speakers it is only about 10 per cent. Increasingly such students have joined social struggles. The wildcat strikes of Limburg coal-miners early in 1970, for instance, were encouraged by students from Louvain, as they had been in February 1968 when two miners were killed in fierce riots. Apart from these troubles, there has been considerable unrest at Brussels, Ghent and Liége Universities also, springing from the same discontents felt in the student world beyond Belgium's frontiers.

In March 1969 for instance, Liége University students occupied the radio and television centre. At Ghent, police invaded the University buildings after students had occupied it for a week; at the same time 2,000 Louvain students marched through Brussels while a hundred of their friends occupied the Ministry of Education. This time it was the French-language students of Louvain who rioted, because of Socialist reluctance to vote the $340 million estimated cost of moving half of this expanding Catholic university, before money had been found for two new state university colleges at Antwerp and Mons.

UNITY OR FEDERALISM

Premier Gaston Eyskens had been elected in 1968 largely on his promise to resolve the constitutional problem of federalism versus unity 'quickly and globally'. But for many months committees, working groups and round tables followed each other with as little success as in previous years. Eyskens was helped by the two Ministers for Community Relations, the Walloon Freddy Terwagne and the Fleming Leo Tindemans. By September 1969 he had created a new all-party working group including the extremists, which achieved some success the following November in outlining a scheme for economic decentralization (for which the Walloon Socialists pressed), linked with cultural autonomy – on which Catholic Flemings insisted. But the problem of Brussels proved again to be the great stumbling block.

Undeterred, Eyskens set up a new group and pledged it would find a solution for Brussels by mid-December. The Volksunie refused to serve in the new group, insisting that the 1963 laws had settled the linguistic pattern for the capital once and for all. M. Vanden Boeynants, the city's most outstanding bilingual politician, also withdrew. It soon appeared that the Flemings in the group had stayed within it on purpose to block any possible 'nibbling away' at the Flemishness of Brussels' six Flemish communes. The French speakers on the other hand were determined that French-language families living in the Flemish boroughs should not be deprived of the natural parental right to have their children educated in their own language in local schools paid for out of local rates. They also rejected the Flemings' claim to a 50–50 share in the administration of the city on the grounds that almost 80 per cent of its population was French-speaking.

After eight more weeks of patient negotiation, Eyskens, on 18 February 1970, at last presented his global plan to the Belgian Lower House. He proposed that the constitution should formally recognize the existence of the Flemish and Walloon communities (as well as the small German-speaking minority along the eastern frontier). Each community would be responsible for its own cultural affairs; the Flemings and Walloons would also have wide powers on regional economic development. As this proposal merely recognized and developed the powers of the Economic and Cultural Councils already in existence, it was largely acceptable. But his proposal for Brussels was more controversial. He suggested the 19 autonomous communes should be given a Greater Brussels Council in which 30 per cent of the seats would be reserved for Flemings. By 1976 they would achieve parity. For cultural affairs the capital would be treated as a miniature Belgium, with a French-language and a Flemish-language cultural council which would also be responsible for schools. Brussels would also have an economic council made up of the two communities.

Premier Eyskens finally proposed a formula to meet Walloon fears of being overruled by the permanent Flemish majority in the House of Representatives, with its 121 Flemings against 91 Walloons. Whenever 75 per cent of either language groups feels a bill to be harmful to its interests, the government must withdraw the bill and reconsider it. If it cannot get 75 per cent approval from each language group at a final reading, the government would have to resign.

Eyskens' next problem was to get the necessary two-thirds majority for his proposals, without which no constitutional changes can become law. However the Liberals always disliked decentralization, and being in opposition were not disposed to co-operate. Yet all the three traditional parties well knew that their delays helped the extremist groups gain ground, and fostered the public sense of disillusion at the frequent stalemate of the central government.

In December 1969 Paul-Henri Spaak had emerged from his political retirement to make an unexpected plea in favour of federalism, after having supported the unitary state throughout his public career. Spaak's proposal was to create a three-way federalist system shared between Flanders, Wallonia and Brussels. Within the capital, he said, power should be divided equally between Flemings and Walloons. The new federal government should share Fleming and Walloon votes equally, and should still control foreign affairs, defence and finance affairs. Other matters should be placed within the competence of new Fleming and Walloon legislatures.

In Spaak's eyes this would give each area linguistic and social satisfactions. Economically the country is too small for such subdivisions to make good sense, but seen in the European context there is a growing link between, say, Walloon Liége, Flemish Limburg and the German Rhine. In the same way, industrialized Flanders is naturally drawn to the highly developed French industries around Lille and Dunkirk. If economic prosperity increasingly ignores frontiers, then Belgium is free to impose whatever linguistic ones she wishes, for in the long run they will not matter.

In the short run, however, the problems remain. For instance, if the Flemish area prospers and the Walloon region continues to decline, how much should the north help the south? Even now, Flanders is poorer than Wallonia in income per head of population. And up to now, as Premier Pierre Harmel complained in 1965, the country has developed the habit of 'buying out political discords at the expense of the public treasury'.

DRAINS ON THE BUDGET

An outstanding example is education. Apart from the vexed case of Louvain University, education is expensive at all levels because the state subsidizes a double network of both Church and lay schools, which involves costly duplication. This was the solution to the four-year schools war, settled in 1958. The pact is due to expire in

1970 and at present it is impossible to foresee economies in the educational budget; the evidence all tends the other way.

The social services are also a drain on the budget; they are mainly run through Catholic or Socialist Friendly Societies, who tend to draw on national treasury funds with little thought of economy, in what are virtually rival bids for political popularity. Attempts to rationalize spending helped to precipitate the big winter strike of 1960–61. They were also a main cause of the doctors' strike which brought Belgium into the world's news headlines in the spring of 1964.

For years the deficit on the health service had grown annually, and the government tried to secure the doctors' help in their efforts to tighten free spending. But doctors complained that government regulations indicated a cheap standard treatment for each category of illness, and that this would both waste their medical skill and also turn them into government agents whose chief duty was filling forms classifying their patients into administrative categories. They also said that there could be no professional secrecy between doctor and patient because of the prying eyes of government clerks. In the eyes of the government, the chief secret that doctors wished to preserve was their own profit. At that time the official rate for a consultation was 100 francs, of which the state repaid 75 francs to the patient through the national health scheme. But the patient probably paid his doctor quite a bit more, perhaps 150 francs, believing that the extra money brought him extra care and attention. The doctor was pleased too, because on his tax return the consultation would be rated at 100 francs and nobody except the individual patient would know exactly how much the doctor had received. But the tax dodging itself cheated the revenue, and indirectly contributed to the high cost of the health service.

On 1 April 10,000 of the country's 12,000 doctors downed instruments and the strike, incredibly, had begun. The government recalled army doctors, but in the end the doctors won. Questions of economy were to be disregarded; and professional secrecy between doctor and patient was to be respected. Once more discord had been bought out at the expense of the treasury. Early in 1966 doctors threatened to strike again over questions of pay increase. They again largely won their claims. Recent governments have included a minister of the budget whose task is to control as closely as possible the accounts of ministries that tend to overspend.

To counter this overspending the government has sharply increased income tax from its previously low level; the bank rate has repeatedly been raised and other taxes have risen, especially those on cigarettes, wines and luxury goods. The Socialists complain that business has got off too lightly. But governments have been reluctant to clamp down on business profits, since industry already finds it difficult to finance its own expansion.

Belgian agriculture is also a drain on the treasury through national subsidies, though national protection is gradually being replaced by the more comprehensive system of the Common Market. About 5 per cent of Belgium's working population are farmers, although there is a constant drift of landworkers into industrial jobs in the towns. In the northern Flemish plains the farms are small, sometimes of even less than three acres, and are almost invariably family concerns, very intensively cultivated, with considerable use of fertilizers but, until recently, less agricultural machinery. Flax, sugar beet, hops, tobacco, cattle, butter and cheese, fruits, cereals, potatoes, cut flowers, plants and market gardening, including early vegetables and asparagus, Belgian chicory (sometimes called endives) and hothouse grapes are all important in the northern areas. The hillier regions of the Ardennes are less fertile; they are specially noted for timber and for pigs, while the country's wheatfields are mostly found in the central areas of Hainaut, Brabant and Hesbaye.

Despite this farm output, Belgium is an importer of foodstuffs. Like Britain, she is a workshop for the world and lives mainly by importing raw materials and exporting finished products – chiefly to her Common Market partners. She has traditionally favoured a low-tariff, free-trading policy. That is why Belgium made the first modest steps towards tariff cutting with the creation of the Benelux union in 1944, and why she enthusiastically joined the Common Market when it was set up in 1958.

BENELUX

The Benelux organization is naturally now somewhat over-shadowed by the European Economic Community, to which Belgium, the Netherlands, and Luxembourg also belong; in any case, Benelux has had a somewhat chequered history since it first came into practical operation in 1948. The two northern neighbours started on terms of great inequality, since the Netherlands had suffered immensely greater war losses than Belgium, in flooded land and devastated, dismantled industries. Moreover, Belgium kept the Congo for many years more, whereas the Dutch lost their Indonesian empire in 1949 after four years' heavy fighting. Most important of all, Belgium and Luxembourg followed a policy of high wages and prices, both of which were strictly controlled at much lower levels in Holland. However, tariff alignment was led gradually towards a Benelux customs union for industrial goods, though Belgian and Luxembourg agriculture remain more heavily protected and less efficient than the Dutch. In 1958, only shortly after the establishment of the European Economic Community, the treaty for a Benelux Economic Union came into existence. According to this transitional agreement the full harmonization of rules and regulations should have been completed by November 1967. When that date came, too little in fact had been achieved, mostly because of the unexpected strength of non-tariff barriers. An example is the sale of pharmaceuticals, of which over 10,000 varieties are sold in Belgium and only 4,500 are licensed in Holland; and who could have known that pornography is distributed on a much less permissive scale in Belgium than in the Netherlands?

In April 1969, Benelux ministers met and agreed to abolish all controls by November 1970 or July 1971 at latest. Some time before, however, new difficulties between the three members had arisen, mainly because of the internal situation in Belgium. In the past many of the Walloons had been among the staunchest supporters of Benelux; nowadays they tend to be wary of increasing the convergence of interest between the Dutch and the Flemish in trade as in language. Undoubtedly Dutch liberal trade policies find more echo in the harbours of Flanders than in the stagnating industrial sectors of

Wallonia. Again, traditional Dutch support for the Atlantic Alliance and for British entry into the Common Market is far stronger than among Francophile Belgian French speakers. One Dutch commentator remarked in 1969, when the Benelux organization celebrated its twenty-fifth anniversary, that in its longish history of half success the Union showed signs of being an old man looking jealously over his shoulder at his child and rival, the Common Market. He also commented that even the latter was not so healthy.[3]

CAPITAL OF EUROPE?

For eleven years the executive commission of the European Common Market occupied a rented building on the Avenue de la Joyeuse Entrée in Brussels. The 5,000 Eurocrats and their cars with 'European' number plates have become a familiar feature of the capital. In 1969 they transferred to the huge Berlaimont administrative centre built especially for them and for the European Atomic Energy Community. The challenge of the Common Market has sharpened the contrast between Belgium's slow rate of economic growth and that of her partners. But it has attracted new activity to the country; apart from all the camp followers of the European organizations, three or four hundred American firms now have offices in the capital. The city is being transformed from a provincial town to a lively international centre. In the words of ex-premier Theo Lefèvre, Brussels is proud to be the 'official candidate for the title of European capital'.

In 1967, after General de Gaulle had given the NATO organization notice to quit its headquarters at Porte Dauphine in Paris, the fourteen members of the Atlantic Alliance accepted the invitation of the Belgian government and decided to transfer their Supreme Headquarters (SHAPE) to Casteau near Mons, about thirty-five miles south-west of Brussels. Socialists and Communists opposed this move; Flemings feared another French-speaking influx and ordinary Belgian citizens were afraid their small country might become the first target in any future war. But nobody protested strongly. Within six months Belgium had not only accepted the newcomers but had also built headquarters at Evere, on the outskirts of Brussels, for the NATO Council and the organization's national delegations.

Yet the arrival of such big delegations inside the heart of the city increases the need to group all Brussels' nineteen autonomous municipalities into one single agglomeration. The administrative inefficiency of changing language from commune to commune, the cost of running nineteen different police forces and many other anomalies seem absurd for a city that seriously aspires to be the capital of Europe. But the only time that Brussels was administered as a single unit was by the Nazi military government during the occupation. 'Grossbrüssel' was patriotically broken up again after the war. Since then, no one seems to have had any creative conception of the city's role.

Some Belgians are now suggesting in all seriousness that English might be accepted as the new *lingua franca* of the city of Brussels and of all Belgium, especially if Britain joins the Common Market. In this way, it is said, the country would be encouraged through its adopted language to widen its horizons and discard the inefficiency that goes with parochialism. Both Flemings and Walloons would have to make efforts to learn the new language. Neither would be favoured, for the Teutonic roots shared between the Dutch and English languages do not help much for practical purposes. And Walloons would have the incentive of learning a tongue that would certainly be worth their effort; as the Swedish sociologist Carl-Hendrik Hojer has pointed out, they persist in believing it is unjust to expect them to learn Flemish.[4]

Yet in the present climate of opinion this solution seems utopian. As we have seen, the language question has penetrated every cranny of national life. It even affected the solidarity of the doctors in 1964, when French-language Socialist physicians broke the strike. And when religious emotions also become involved, as over the Louvain question, sparks are certain to fly. Where his faith, culture and language are all concerned, every Belgian is capable of becoming an extremist.

15 On 22 July 1950 King Leopold returned to Belgium after six years of exile. Despite a majority vote in favour of his return, the country exploded into riots, strikes and street fighting.

16   17

16 Paul-Henri Spaak, Belgium's internationally known postwar statesman, was first president of the UN General Assembly.
17 Françoise Mallet-Joris, author of the best-selling *Maison de Papier*, won the Femina Prize in 1958 with *Empire Céleste*.

18 Georges Simenon, creator of the Inspector Maigret series of 'psychological' detective stories and author of over 200 works.
19 Surrealist master René Magritte, at work in his studio.

18

20 Baudouin, King of the Belgians, and Queen Fabiola at the Palace of Laeken. King Baudouin came to the throne on 17 July 1951 when his father was forced to abdicate.

21 Prince Charles, brother of ex-king Leopold III, greets veterans of the Resistance. He himself went into hiding with the Maquis forces in the Ardennes, and later acted as Regent during King Leopold's exile.

22 The giant electrical and electronics works of ACEC at Charleroi
in Hainaut. Above: six 155,000 kVA super-cooled alternators under
construction.

23 Flower-growing is also big business in Belgium. Opposite: a
field of begonias at Lochristi, East Flanders.

24, 25 Above: the flat, drained polder land praised by Flemish poets such as Emile Verhaeren. Below: the Ardennes, which Belgians like to believe was Shakespeare's Forest of Arden.

26 Opposite: the Tower of Dixmude, symbol and rallying-point of Flemish nationalism, displays the cross-shaped letters implying 'All for Flanders, Flanders for Christ'.

27 The French-speaking Walloons, like the Flemings, love pageantry and festival. Above: the Shrove Tuesday carnival of the 'Gilles' at Binche.

28 Carrefour de l'Europe – the Crossroads of Europe – and the Eurocrat's car with the EUR registration are symbols of Brussels' place as headquarters of the Common Market.

10 Business, Church and State

BELGIUM'S BUSINESS CONCENTRATION dates back even before independence, to 1822 when Dutch William founded the great centre of industrial wealth, the Société Générale. At the present day the Société is estimated to have direct control over about 20 per cent of Belgian industry and indirect control over a great deal more, quite apart from its still dominant position in certain areas of the Congo. The Société Générale runs approximately 30 per cent of all coal production, 40 per cent of iron and steel, 90 per cent of non-ferrous metals and 25 per cent of electricity, together with half of all banking deposits and insurance. There are small shareholders all over Belgium who hold stock in the Société or its many dependencies. In the past, the top management of the Société has been predominantly Walloon and Catholic, though it has increasingly recruited gifted Flemings into its team. Its working language is French.

Apart from the Société there are a number of smaller but powerful similar companies, particularly the long-established family groups such as Coupée, Empain, Solvay, Lambert and Nagelmaekers, who together control many of the traditional industries as well as glass, chemicals, and cement, and a smaller proportion of the newer industries such as oil and petroleum products, electrical equipment, and other consumer goods.

Since the second world war Belgium's growth rate has been mediocre, and the big trusts and holding companies have not been in the vanguard of the recent great drive to diversify production. They have been criticized for this prudence, which is indeed somewhat surprising at first sight, since the broad spread of their investments would appear to make it possible to switch financial resources to companies that need new capital, leaving the risk well-cushioned. Some Belgians explain that growth products are usually too heavily protected to allow large Belgian sales abroad, while Belgium herself is too small to produce profitably for the home market alone. Instead, effort has been concentrated on the modernization of existing old industries. The position has changed somewhat for the better with the opening of the Common Market; but in the meantime, short of a large home market, the Belgian trusts invested heavily abroad, particularly in the Congo and more recently in Canada.

The Banque Nationale de Belgique, Belgium's central bank, has had exclusive authority to issue banknotes for Belgium since 1873, and for the Belgo-Luxembourg Economic Union since 1921. The bank remains an autonomous joint-stock company, still involved in profit-making banking activities; but its chief concern has become the technical management of the currency and the safeguarding of monetary stability by regulating the supply of credit and the country's external reserves. It is obliged by statute to keep a gold reserve equivalent to one-third of its sight liabilities, although in practice this is usually nearer to 50 per cent. To cover the rest of the note circulation, the bank must hold easily realizable assets. It is the government's banker, and lends to the government, although its advances are limited to a ceiling of 10 milliard francs.

The three biggest commercial banks of Belgium are the Société Générale de Banque, the Banque de Bruxelles and the Kredietbank. The latter has branches in Brussels and throughout the Flemish provinces, but not in the Walloon areas; it has, however, agreements with other banks serving the Walloon region. Until the great depression of the 1930s Belgian banks were important shareholders in industrial companies, but in 1934 the van Zeeland government forbade the banks to hold shares in enterprises other than banking companies, although their lending to industry was not restricted. Now banks are required to lend a certain proportion of their capital to the government for the financing of the national debt.

An unusually developed service of Belgian banks is the provision of safe deposits for rent, usually to hold the securities which are very widely owned among all sections of the population – quite often by people with no bank account at all. In recent years the deposit banks have made a great drive to recruit small savers, in competition with the very efficient post-office cheque or 'giro' system. This is Belgium's most popular way of paying small bills, especially regular accounts for gas, electricity, telephones, and so on. Such bills are paid at the post office, in cash or by post-office cheque. No interest is paid on post-office cheque accounts, but the system is widely used because of its ease and efficiency.

THE TRADE UNIONS

About two-thirds of all Belgium's manual and white-collar workers belong to trade unions; women workers are the least 'unionized'. There is a good deal of political rivalry between the Catholic and Socialist unions, although their economic aims are very similar. The Socialists have often been more ready to use the strike weapon than the Catholic unions. In industrial life, the unions have considerable power; Catholics and Socialists sit together with the employers on the works councils. They negotiate agreements, fixing wages and productivity for a set number of years. Such agreements are usually respected by both sides: there are few wildcat strikes. Except in the case of the coal-mines, the unions have raised little objection in the past to rationalization programmes, agreeing that productivity must rise if wages rise, even at the cost of some redundancy. This attitude is being put to sterner test now that automation is developing faster.

The unions believe that owners will ultimately have to share part of their authority, as absolute monarchs have given way to constitutional government. At present they are very far from that, although on the national level a National Labour Council and a Central Council for the Economy advise parliament, respectively, on the social and economic questions that concern labour.

Trade-union officials in Belgium are trained for their job in a somewhat haphazard way; most shop stewards attend part-time courses or summer schools. More recently, the unions have recruited economists and sociologists with university degrees, even though such officials are not expected to have worked on the shop floor.

Industrial wages and most white-collar salaries are tied to the retail price index. The working week is usually of less than forty-five hours, worked in five days. There is a statutory annual holiday of three weeks, with full pay and a holiday bonus equal to three weeks' salary as well. At present, there are insufficient skilled workers in Belgium; the government is seeking to remedy this by technical training courses for young workers, and by family allowance to the age of twenty-one or twenty-four for apprentices or students.

The legal obligations imposed on employers often surprise foreign business men who start new enterprises in Belgium. The country is at the opposite extreme from the American 'hire and fire' system. The period of notice for white-collar workers is very long and varies according to the level of salary and of responsibility. In addition, a law was introduced in 1960 making it necessary to pay compensation to workers made redundant by the closure of their firms.

The two biggest groups of unions are the Catholic Confederation of Christian Trade Unions, or CSC, and the Socialist General Trade Union Federation (FGTB). They are now pressing for four weeks' paid leave plus an allowance equal to four weeks' salary per year.

Belgium has about 250,000 foreign workers, most of them Italians, Greeks, Spaniards, North Africans and Turks. The more recent newcomers are not unionized; they were at the heart of the long wildcat strike of Limburg coalminers early in 1970, which the big unions opposed. Most migrant workers are intent on earning as much cash as possible so as to return to their own countries after a few years. They are therefore less interested in fringe benefits and their priorities sometimes clash with those of local workers. This, in Belgium as elsewhere, has led to a climate of suspicion between migrant and native workers.

The country's social security system was worked out in its present form at the end of the second world war, and was made even more generous in the 1950s under the Socialist-led coalition of Achille Van Acker. It includes holiday and family allowances and maternity benefits as well as unemployment pay and pensions for old age, sickness and disablement. It is principally the two latter that have recently made such demands on the Treasury as to force the government to take measures to curb spending. The social security scheme is not administered by the state but by the trade unions' benefit societies, the unions in turn being closely linked to the political parties. Employers pay about half the theoretical cost of the service, workers one quarter and the state the other quarter – or more, when it runs into deficit. This now occurs in most years.

THE PARTIES

The *Christian Social Party* has tried to reduce its confessional links since it was reconstituted from the old Catholic party after World War II. It now includes a small minority which belongs to other creeds or to no creed, but it remains essentially the Catholic party that has been a major force in Belgian political life throughout the country's independent existence. It recruits many of its voters in Flanders, especially among the small-town workers, almost all of whom also belong to the Confédération des Syndicats Chrétiens, or Confederation of Christian Trade Unions. This has over 900,000 members and is in turn linked with the Jeunesse Ouvrière Chrétienne (Young Christian Workers) and the Alliance des Mutualités Chrétiennes, or Alliance of Christian Benefit Societies. All of these are more left-wing than other sections of the party, and against the resistance of the conservative elements constantly force party policy into rival bids with the Socialists in gaining advantages for workers. The party's right-wingers include most of Belgium's older aristocracy, some of the great banking or business firms, and the Fédération des Classes Moyennes (the artisans and small shopkeepers), many white-collar workers and above all the farming classes of both the Flemish and Walloon rural areas. The Boerenbond, or Flemish Peasants' League, has long been the firm backbone of the party; in contrast with it, the Walloon Alliance Agricole plays a minor role. As these different groups are bound to each other only by religious feeling and otherwise often have conflicting interests, common action is frequently difficult. The numerical dominance of Flemings within the party has also led to disharmony, although the extremists have now mostly left to join the Volksunie. The language dispute has gravely shaken the party's traditional support for a unitary state.

The Socialist Party dropped its old name of Parti Ouvrier Belge to call itself the Parti Socialiste Belge in 1945 when it was reconstituted after the war. It is the most homogeneous of Belgium's three traditional parties, coming as it does predominantly from the single class of the once-downtrodden but now powerful workers. Its main strength has always been in the Walloon centres of heavy industry; it also has strong appeal in the bigger cities of Flanders such as Antwerp, Ghent, Bruges, Malines and Louvain. The official programme of the Socialist party still pays lip-service to Marxism, but history has shown it to be prudent and reformist in its day-to-day attitudes. At the same time, memories of the bad old days help explain the rooted Socialist dislike of big business, especially of the powerful holding companies which are suspected of neglecting Belgian interests. 'They are too big to be patriotic', is a characteristic Socialist gibe. Socialist propaganda has been most extremist when, as between the world wars and immediately after them, Communists have captured part of the workers' vote. The Fédération Générale du Travail de Belgique, the Socialist trade-union federation, has always been under pressure to be more extreme than the party itself, especially from the militant Walloon left-wing groups.

The big strike during the winter of 1960 was almost entirely a Socialist affair, and was launched in the first place by the unions without party consent. It justified the fears of its critics who see the Socialists as a revolutionary party. Such critics called Paul-Henri Spaak, who returned from the secretary-generalship of NATO to take government office after the strike, 'the false nose of respectability on the revolutionary monster'.

The Socialist party is anticlerical, although the parish registers of Liége, a Socialist stronghold, show that 95 per cent of its inhabitants are baptized and that 80 per cent of them receive Christian burial. The socialists have also been much influenced throughout their history by French thought. During General de Gaulle's reign their pro-French sympathies sometimes tinged Belgian Socialist views with Gaullism; they care less for President Pompidou, mostly because of his past connections with big business.

The Socialist party favours a unitary state with considerable decentralization, leaving Walloons to plan their own future but with the right to block legislation considered against their economic interests. In 1961, after the big strike, a new pressure group for federalism arose, called the Mouvement Populaire Wallon. Linked with the Socialist trade unions, this attracted many recruits among Walloons deeply anxious about their future. The Mouvement claimed that the old economic need for unity between the two halves of Belgium no longer applied, and that as the barriers between Common Market countries gradually came down, their area would fit well into the larger whole of a federal or confederal Europe. For some time, relations between the MPW and the Socialist Party were strained on the federal issue and other questions. At the Tournai Congress in the spring of 1967 a great effort was made by all Walloon Socialist groups to sink their differences and to close ranks in face of their deteriorating economic situation. By the elections of the following year some Walloon Socialists had left to join one of the French-language splinter groups; while in the capital and in the Flemish area, Flemish and French-language candidates rivalled each other for Socialist votes by presenting separate lists.

The *Party of Liberty and Progress* has been the name, since 1961, of the old Liberal party. In that year it broadened its programme by trying to shake off the traditional anticlericalism which had been one of the main characteristics of the old Liberals right up to the end of the schools 'war' in 1958. Its old links with Freemasonry and with Belgium's small Jewish community still exist, but are not dominant; in 1961 the new PLP stressed its religious tolerance in an attempt to capture the votes of Catholics who were dissatisfied by the dominance of the workers within their own party. Essentially it has inherited the political conservatism and economic liberalism of the nineteenth-century Liberal party. It still believes in free trade, low taxes, the limitation of government spending and a minimum of state control of industry. It is very much a middle-class party, attracting voters from industry, finance and the professions. In the elections of May 1965 it drew a number of Socialist votes, and still cherishes hopes of forming a great centre party although in recent years the increasing importance of Belgium's language question has caused it to lose votes to new splinter groups. The party emphasizes the joint economic interests that should bind Flemings and Walloons together, and does not support the movement towards federalism. Originally the Liberal party opposed the rise of the Flemish movement. It is still a mainly French-language party, but has valuable recruits from the Flemish-speaking middle classes, especially in Antwerp. Liberal trade unions have about 100,000 members; but unlike the two bigger political parties, Liberalism never developed extensive social clubs. It claims to be the natural defender of independent workers. Though always small in size, the Liberal party has held office in a majority of twentieth-century coalitions, and has often been a fulcrum of parliamentary life, owing to its power to give the casting vote. Nowadays its key importance has been shaken by the rise of the new fringe groups.

Of the smaller parties, *Communism* is now no longer important, especially as it is divided within itself between supporters of Moscow and of Peking. The *Volksunie* has been gaining support ever since it won its first two seats in the 1958 elections. It represents the extremist fringe of Flemish separatism and has been very active in Louvain, Brussels and all other recent trouble spots. It is fired by a burning sense of past injustices, which leads it to adopt language that to onlookers sometimes seems excessive, as for instance its complaint that Flanders has been 'intellectually and materially crippled ... slaughtered ... a case of mental genocide'.[1]

The *Rassemblement Wallon* first presented itself at the 1968 elections as a Walloon answer to the Volksunie. It includes Socialists, Liberals and some Catholics from the latter's older Walloon splinter group the Renovation Wallonne. The party won four seats in the 1968 elections.

The French-speaking *Front Démocratique des Francophones* was formed mainly among Brussels voters, to act as a pressure group against the 1963 laws on the linguistic boundaries, which were – and still are – seen as grossly unjust to French-speaking Brussels commuters. It won three seats in the 1965 elections and since then has often linked with the Rassemblement Wallon in defence of French-language interests.

PARLIAMENT

In Belgium, after a general election, the business of choosing a government begins. Neither of the two main parties is big enough these days to win outright, so almost all governments are coalitions composed of two of the three groups: Catholics, Socialists and Liberals. Belgians have lived for fifty years with the combinations of the three-party system and show little sign of active change. The recent growth of small extremist parties only serves to make the work of the coalitions more difficult, but voters become accustomed to frequent government immobility. The coalitions can take very long to form – as in 1968, when 132 days elapsed before the Eyskens Christian Social–Socialist government was agreed.

King Baudouin begins post-election activities by appointing an *informateur* to sound out all three main parties so as to pick a man capable of forming an acceptable dosage of different interests into the new team. Party leaders are not seen as automatic choices. When he has found a likely man, the *informateur* hands over to a *formateur*, i.e. to the potential new premier. He may have to tell the King he cannot form a coalition, in which case the King himself appoints another *formateur*. This gives the King some effective powers at election time. Similarly, if a coalition breaks down, the King again first appoints an *informateur* and then a *formateur* so that a new cabinet may be created without new elections. Or he may refuse to accept the resignation of the outgoing premier and simply tell him and his team to return to work.

King Baudouin, like his father, now uses these powers to the full. Again like Leopold in the 1930s, Baudouin in recent years has condemned the parties' tendency to make deals outside the parliamentary framework, thus reducing parliament's real power. The nation accepts his influence, and seems to appreciate having a permanent referee who indeed does a great deal of work in settling disputes, and is accepted as being *au dessus de la mêlée*. The position of the Belgian monarchy is a remarkable phenomenon; in contrast with the more illustrious houses of Habsburg, Romanov or Hohenzollern, the Saxe-Coburgs have shown great powers of survival; perhaps they are indeed indispensable.

The two Belgian houses of parliament are the House of Representatives of 212 seats, and the Senate. The latter has 178 members, 106 of whom are voted for at elections while the rest are co-opted or chosen by the nine provincial councils. Elections fall due every four years, and are always held on Sundays. Voting is compulsory.

DEFENCE

After June 1940 the Belgian army largely ceased to exist, apart from units attached to the Allied forces exiled in Great Britain. When the army was re-formed in 1946 it naturally possessed very little equipment; right up to 1960 the United States supplied most of the bigger weapons under the military assistance programme. In 1949 Belgium joined the Atlantic Alliance. By the time of the Korean war in the early 1950s Belgium had a fairly high rate of defence expenditure, approximating to 5 per cent of the gross national product. But in the second half of that decade, like other small NATO countries, Belgium cut this down to below 4 per cent, and also reduced the length of military service from two years to twenty-one months, which was in turn cut to eighteen months, then fifteen, and finally to twelve months, where it now stands. This accorded with Belgium's traditional dislike of the military career, linked with the long tradition of neutrality, and even more to popular dislike of conscription and military spending.

Since Belgium's withdrawal from the Congo in 1960 her defence planning has been geared to European requirements. In terms of her 9½ million population, Belgium now has the smallest defence expenditure in NATO and also the smallest defence-related industries. She has produced small arms, mines and rockets for some time, most of this growing out of her traditional small-arms industry centred round Liége. Also, by 1960 the electronics and aerospace companies began to secure defence contracts for repair and overhaul, for instance, of the jet engines Belgium had begun to produce under licence from Britain. In 1968 Belgium bought French Mirage V jets to replace old American equipment, mainly because of generous French terms for a share in the production and maintenance of the aircraft.

The Ateliers de Construction Electriques de Charleroi (ACEC) handles much of the limited electronic contract work. Another firm is Bell Telephones (which Paul-Henri Spaak joined when he left the diplomatic service in 1966); this is a subsidiary of International Telephone and Telegraph, which is the biggest electronics company in Belgium. Tanks are not made in the country. There is virtually no spending in Belgium on military research and development, except for small arms. The NATO standard rifle is the FN automatic, made in Liége and perhaps the most successful effort at standardization in the whole Atlantic Alliance.

Belgium now has a small but good air force consisting of seven fighter-bomber, interceptor and reconnaissance squadrons assigned to NATO, and also one transport wing. Her major land forces are two mechanized divisions also assigned to NATO and stationed in West Germany, plus a paracommando regiment. Belgium's missile force consists of Honest John rockets and launchers, Nike Ajax surface-to-air missiles and Hawk anti-aircraft missiles, most of them obtained from the United States. Her small navy consists of minesweepers, coastal escorts and support ships.

In 1957 Paul-Henri Spaak succeeded Lord Ismay as Secretary-General of NATO, just before the successful launching of the first Russian sputnik forced NATO to consider global defence. Spaak's views on such problems were published in 1959 in English in a Penguin Special called *Why NATO?* Belgian Foreign Minister Pierre Harmel in turn put forward a plan in December 1966 to use the NATO organization for wider political co-operation between its members, particularly to foster East–West *détente*. His 'Alliance for Peace' plan included possible reciprocal troop reductions by NATO and Warsaw Pact members.

Since 1967 the 8,000 staff of the Supreme Headquarters for Allied Powers in Europe (SHAPE) have been housed on the site of a former Belgian army camp at Casteau-Masière near Mons.

THE PRESS
The great diversity of the Belgian press testifies to the country's continuing attachment to local and regional interests. The chief

dailies in Flemish are the *Belang van Limburg, De Nieuwe Gids, Het Laatste Nieuws* and *De Standaard* of Brussels, *Het Volk* of Ghent, and in Antwerp, the Socialist *Volksgazet* and the Christian Social *Gazet van Antwerpen*. French-language dailies include the right-wing Catholic *Libre Belgique*, the Socialist *Le Peuple*, the Liberal *Dernière Heure* and *Le Soir*, an independent evening paper and by far the best of the French-language dailies. The weeklies *Pourquoi Pas* and *Spécial* are widely read, as well as *Pan*, a satirical sheet that models itself on the French *Canard Enchaîné*. *Ons Land* and *De Post* appear to have the biggest sales among Flemish weeklies; however, it is not the practice for Belgian publications to reveal their circulation figures. Among the best monthlies are *De Maand, De Vlaamse Gids*, the *Revue Générale Belge* and the *Revue Nouvelle*. Other publications include a number of pigeon-fanciers' magazines with a total estimated circulation of 200,000, a Pink Journal printed in Flemish and French which lists the marriage banns published in all the communes, and a Poet's Paper of a respectable literary quality.

Belgium has no press censorship or Press Council but, like France, offers offended readers the right of reply to any report in which they believe they have been unjustly dealt with. They have the right to send the paper an answer up to twice the length of the original article, and the paper is obliged to print it in the same size of type and on the same page as the original allegations. Dailies do not print readers' letters to the editor; this kind of public forum for the airing of grievances or presentation of ideas is little known.

Only in January 1966 did it become necessary to deposit a copy of all publications appearing in Belgium with the Brussels Royal Library.

THE CHURCH
According to the constitution, four creeds – Roman Catholic, Evangelical, Anglican and Jewish – have equal recognition in Belgium. The Anglicanism was included because Leopold I had adopted that faith while married to Princess Charlotte of England. About 85 per cent of the population belongs to the Catholic religion, and more than half of them are practising Catholics.

The Catholic Church is wealthy and powerful. Its openly political role in national life was typified throughout the career of the late Archbishop of Malines, Cardinal van Roey, who died in 1961. He was noted for his fervent support for Leopold III over the abdication issue. His frequent condemnation of strikes was a source of embarrassment to the left wing of the Catholic party. Parish priests tend to speak equally openly on political matters and are also active in Catholic economic and social groups. The priest is often a recruiting officer for Catholic trade unions, as well as traditionally being treasurer of the local branch of the Boerenbond or Peasants' Union.

It is only in recent years that the Church's control over the faithful has begun to decline, in Belgium as almost everywhere. To some extent the Church is a link that helps lessen the division between the northern and southern halves of the country. But its influence can also work the other way. It was a Flemish priest, Guido Gezelle, who virtually founded the Flemish movement in the nineteenth century and his successors, while championing the Flemish cause, have often condemned all things French and warned their flocks against contamination even by their Walloon neighbours. The importance of the Church in political life has inevitably stimulated anticlericalism among people of opposite political views. This was shown very remarkably in November 1962 in Liége – a region anticlerical right from the centuries in which it was ruled by an archbishop. Local and even national passions became violently aroused over the trial of a Liége woman who had destroyed her week-old daughter, grossly malformed because the mother had taken thalidomide drugs during her pregnancy. The clash of opinion between Catholic orthodoxy and the anticlerical majority in the Liége province before the woman's acquittal even shook the government, at that time the uneasy coalition led by Catholic Premier Théo Lefèvre and Socialist Paul-Henri Spaak.

The present Archbishop of Malines-Brussels, Cardinal Joseph Suenens, first came to international notice as a moderate reformer during the Second Vatican Council. He achieved greater fame after an interview in May 1969 with the French review *Informations Catholiques Internationales*, in which he called for a complete updating

161

of the Roman Curia and for bishops to be allowed more part in decision-making. He urged the election of the Pope by representatives of the whole Church, including the laity, and said that at present the Pope was 'rather the successor of emperors and political sovereigns than of Peter'. Though his remarks were not well received in Rome, he has since become one of the most respected leaders of the reform movement within Catholicism. His book *Co-Responsibility in the Church* sums up the plea of most Catholic liberals: to speak out but stay in the Church.

Another Belgian churchman well known outside his country was Father Georges Pire, who won the 1958 Nobel Peace Prize for his work in settling refugees on the German-Belgian frontier after the second world war. Later, Father Pire founded the Gandhi International Centre at Huy in the Meuse valley, where young people of all races and creeds study the problems of peace and the roots of enmity between nations. In 1960, nine years before his death, he founded a rural community in East Pakistan which later developed into a centre of 30,000 persons who learned to develop their own localities with the help of an international team of specialists.

'ASSOCIATIONISME'

Since the independent existence of Belgium began, Belgian life has been 'politicized' in the sense that practically every citizen is labelled and known to be a member of the Catholic party, or a Liberal, or a Socialist. An independent citizen without party affiliation is a great rarity, and in any case would be speedily classified by his opinions, his origins, and his milieu. Consequently most social or cultural activities are arranged by Catholics or Socialists or, less frequently, Liberals – or by committees comprising a careful mixture of Catholics and non-Catholics, Flemings and Walloons, provincials and townspeople, and so on. 'Not only the law and the army, but writers, artists, and even the most hermetic scientific societies are subject to this departmentalization,' Belgium's Political Science Institute recently reported.

If this is true of the professional classes, it is even more characteristic of the bulk of the population. Both the Socialist and the Catholic parties have developed an enormous network of services that touch economic and social life at almost every point – very many of them, like the social services, aided by state funds. For instance, a child may be born in a Socialist maternity hospital, attend a Socialist paediatric clinic in infancy, and later proceed to Socialist-run nursery, primary, and secondary lay schools. He can enjoy vacations in Socialist holiday homes, join Socialist boy scout or football or cycling clubs. When he is grown up he will join an appropriate Socialist trade union, shop at a Socialist co-operative, and even join a Socialist-run brass band or archery group (very popular in Belgium) or pigeon-racing club. Much of all this network will also have close links with his job, his commune, his province and certainly his language. The corresponding Catholic network is even more complete; so it is perfectly possible for young Belgians to grow up without any great acquaintance with people outside their own enveloping mesh, especially since the entire nation seems passionately fond of clubs, groups, and societies. It is true that affluent modern life has brought a slackening of these links. Even so, a change of political allegiance is a big step for any Belgian. It will involve a change in social habits, and it could even mean a change of job: Belgian communes, which jealously guard their great local autonomy, reflect in miniature the dissensions in national political life, so that the appointment of a local schoolmistress or even of a bus-driver can be a political act.

This clannishness has direct repercussions, conversely, on national politics in Belgium. Already, allegiance to the three main political parties has excluded big swings of opinion, so that the country is obliged to govern itself by coalition, without the clear Ins and Outs of the British or American systems. 'How can you see-saw on a three-legged stool?' Belgians ask. Policies are made even less clear-cut by the need to hold a careful balance within every government between the innumerable pressure groups: not only between Flemings and Walloons and Catholics and non-Catholics, but between rival groups inside the Catholic and Socialist parties, between Brussels and the provinces, between free-traders and farm protectionists, between the professions and the workers, between workers in the old industries and workers in the new, between big business and small independents, between countless rival communes. This means that each coalition must contain not necessarily the most talented men available but the most representative of each group. It also produces large, unwieldy cabinets; and it certainly causes too many delays, stalemates and deadlocks in parliamentary life. Sometimes government immobility has led to the bypassing of normal parliamentary procedure through the use of royal decrees with the force of law, as the only way of acting on important or urgent issues.

11 Culture, countryside and the American connection

DO BELGIANS EXIST, or are there only Flemings and Walloons? Tradition claims that there have always been great differences of temperament between the two linguistic groups. Flemings are said to be taciturn, self-contained, tenacious, obstinate, down-to-earth, vigorous, and yet deeply mystical and naturally religious. The Walloon is regarded as quicker, more nimble, wittier; more spontaneous though more superficial; wily, rather boastful, versatile, sceptical; headstrong rather than tenacious, shallower but more subtle than the Fleming.

This, at least, is how the two groups see each other; but foreigners looking from the outside have not been nearly so aware of Belgian differences as of their similarities. All Belgians, according to one of their own writers, share 'energy and aptitude for work whether it is rough or delicate. Their passion for collective independence and for individual liberty is often mixed with immense attachment to tradition and custom. Their jovial and unbuttoned good nature is sometimes vulgar, and shows itself especially in their delight in the pleasures of the table, in their love of meetings and of public festivals, and of colourful and noisy processions.'[1] The author might also have added that all Belgians are fanatical about their personal independence from officialdom and administration. They use enormous ingenuity and persistence to get round rules and regulations, with an enjoyment in pitting their wits against those of the authorities that is common to peoples who have experienced centuries of foreign rule.

In one sense at least, seeing the Belgians in the round is not difficult: most of them are plump. They eat copiously ('we don't think a meal is worth starting unless there's a lot' a Belgian girl told me); food is always of good quality and well cooked, and Belgians are so fond of all that is succulent and delicious that it is hard to say what is the national dish. Perhaps it is the beefsteak, served with *pommes frites* or French-fried potatoes – the latter so popular that during wartime blackouts, Allied aircraft were said to know whenever they flew over a Belgian town by the all-pervading smell of fried potatoes. Today you can still find *frites* sold at almost every street corner, to be eaten with a hard-boiled egg or a meatball, or with gherkins, pickles, mayonnaise; but strange as it seems to British visitors, never with fish.

Beer is the drink that usually washes down the beefsteak and *frites*. Belgians consume more beer than anybody else in Europe except the Germans. Cafés serving beer are open all day long, and also offer coffee, tea and wine – but not liquor such as whisky; people who prefer the stronger stuff must join a club or drink it at home. For special occasions everybody drinks wine, although the country itself produces scarcely any. Southern Belgium chiefly imports Burgundian wines; they have been sent by road and river from the Dijon area of France ever since the fifteenth-century Dukes of Burgundy ruled Belgium. Walloons are France's best foreign customer for Burgundian wines; while Flemings chiefly import, as they have done for centuries, the clarets that come by sea from Bordeaux to the northern ports, mainly Antwerp. But every kind of drinkable wine is available throughout Belgium – often more reasonably priced than in France; even supermarkets keep good-quality wines as well as cheaper stocks.

Beer, however, remains the customary daily drink for the average Belgian, whether Fleming or Walloon. Almost all Belgian beers are lager-type and are now mostly mass-produced, although faithful local clienteles make some smaller brews commercially successful. Two of the best-known are the half-wheat, half-barley, fermented Gueuze and Lambic, and the reddish cherry-flavoured beer known as Kriek, so bitter that it is usually drunk through a sugar lump.

To foreign onlookers it seems strange that Belgium's preoccupation with good living concerns itself mainly with the inner man and less with his material surroundings. Throughout their country, historic buildings remind Belgians of their outstanding architectural traditions. Yet present-day standards of architecture are mediocre or worse, with a few honourable exceptions such as the Champs des Manœuvres housing development at Liége, or the government information office building at Rue Montoyer in Brussels (the nearby premises of the Banque Lambert are outstandingly good but were designed by American architects). True, the residential suburbs around Brussels contain pleasant-looking villas and apartment blocks; but the vast majority of office buildings in all the big cities look particularly characterless in this country of flamboyantly confident design; and the little houses that grow like mushrooms everywhere are often both ugly and ill-matched.

However, houses and streets whether old or recently built are almost always well cared for and above all, clean. A familiar sight anywhere in Belgium is the housewife with water and broom, sluicing the pavement in front of her house at least once a week. Winter snow is shovelled away with the same zeal; householders have an extra incentive for this, for they are held responsible at law if any passer-by should slip on the stretch of sidewalk in front of their house.

Women are the guardians of the home in Belgium as anywhere, but they are also powers in their own right – as anywhere. Married women are still legally under the control of their husbands; only within the last few years have they gained the right to own separate bank accounts. Yet the family respects their business acumen, as I once learned by direct experience when my husband and I met a Belgian couple to discuss leasing an apartment they owned. During an hour of polite routine haggling, the Belgian lady did all the talking, while her husband brandished his veto in silence. Significantly, their teen-age daughter also sat in on the interview, presumably to learn how mother did it.

There are of course women in public life: writers, doctors, lawyers, a few members of parliament; but on the whole the legal code which considered them as chattels to be guarded by their menfolk has left traces in present-day attitudes, sometimes revealed in unconscious ways. Recently, two young wives from the United States Embassy in Brussels invited a few other women to lunch. The Belgian guests accepted with pleasure, and duly arrived – with their husbands. It had simply not crossed their minds that ladies might lunch alone together.

Only a small proportion of Belgian women seem to take an active interest in politics. Though voting is compulsory, the political pattern has changed little since women were given the full vote in 1949. Women are usually more regular church-goers than their husbands, even in the traditionally religious Flemish north. Catholic husbands, however, see to it that their children are given a Catholic education. If the husband is active in one of the Catholic political groups, he is likely also to carry a banner or a candle in the frequent processions round the parish, or else he may zestfully blow a horn with the accompanying brass band.

Processions, usually religious in origin, are the chief feature of the local festivities which have survived in many Belgian towns both small and large. While there are few national heroes and little national folklore, the country is thick with local customs, hardy witnesses to the strength of local patriotism. Some of the ceremonies of the Flemish *kermis* and the Walloon *ducasse* go back to pre-Christian times. The curious cat festival celebrated each year at Ypres, for example, apparently originated when local Flemings were christianized and gave up their belief in the old Nordic cult of Freya, the goddess who went to war in a chariot drawn by cats. The converts showed their zeal by throwing live cats down from the town belfry. Nowadays stuffed cats have softened that old cruel custom; but they represent a living tradition. Another remarkable Flemish festival is purely Christian: the procession of the Holy Blood at Bruges, which commemorates the year 1150 when the Count of Flanders, Thierry d'Alsace, brought back from a Crusade some drops of blood believed to be Christ's. Once a year this blood is displayed to the people, as the climax of a magnificent procession attended by the archbishop and clergy, in which the Catholic groups of Bruges stage tableaux showing scenes from the Old Testament and from Christ's passion.

South of Brussels in the Walloon town of Binche, the strange carnival of the Gilles attracts crowds who throng the streets every Shrove Tuesday. The Gilles are men of Binche who don, for the great day, elaborate tunics and pants that may have been handed down as family heirlooms for generations; but the most striking and valuable part of the costume is the headdress, which is made of yard-long ostrich plumes. Around their waists they wear belts with tinkling bells, and each man carries a basket full of oranges. They dance down the streets to music that becomes more and more frenetic, pelting the spectators with oranges until dancers and crowd finally mingle in a kind of mass delirium that has to be seen to be believed; of course the celebration also includes gargantuan eating and vast drinking of beer. The festival is said to have originated in the sixteenth century when Mary of Hungary wished to honour her visiting nephew, Philip of Spain, by re-enacting the Spanish conquest of Peru, with the Gilles representing the sixteenth-century idea of Incas.

Near to Binche, at Mons, there is an annual *ducasse* in which a giant St George fights and inflicts a regulation defeat upon a giant dragon. Giants, indeed, are an almost indispensable feature of any procession; very often they are men on stilts who walk miles this way, proud of their bizarre and lofty skill. Another historical procession with a difference is the annual pilgrimage that several Walloon groups make to Waterloo; not, strangely enough, in tribute to the Duke of Wellington and the Allied troops who ended Napoleon's drain of Belgian men and money, but to deplore Napoleon's defeat. This sentiment is not shared by the Flemings, who consider Napoleon as an enemy because of his disregard for Flemish culture.

ROUND TRIP

British visitors arriving on the Flemish coast often show their ignorance of Belgium's language problems by trying out their stumbling French on the local people. But these days the question is forced on the notice of even the most inattentive and unconcerned holidaymakers – indeed many Frenchmen have been discouraged from coming after finding their cars damaged, the French-language masses in Ostend churches disturbed by noisy Flemish demonstrators, and windows of French-speaking shops broken, with advertisements ripped out. However, local tradespeople strongly oppose such violence, and it is still possible for tourists to understand nothing as long as they stay on the coast's wide and crowded sandy beaches. Yet a little exploration would be richly rewarding, by giving visitors some understanding not only of the language divisions but of the varied nature of the country, in its beauty, its ugliness and its troubled soul.

Looking south beyond the grey sea and the golden sands, one sees the flat polder land of Flanders, soon merging into the wide Flemish plain with church belfries standing sharp against the skyline in a landscape broken up into tiny fields, often no bigger than kitchen gardens. During most mornings and evenings, a luminous misty haze envelops them, rising from innumerable drainage channels. Around the old medieval villages modern buildings have spread until the wide plain seems a spider's web of interlocking streets and houses, neither town nor true countryside. Often, single houses stand alone among the fields, tall and thin with two blank side walls, as if they had been sliced off from an imaginary terrace. Such 'slices of cake' as the Dutch call them are built like this because their owners cannily foresee that, one day, neighbours will build next to them and will pay quite heavily to join up to one of the blank walls. At the present rapid rate of housebuilding, not much time elapses before the single house becomes one of many, along the length of a new road.

Farther to the east the countryside changes. For centuries the Kempenland, or Campine, was one of the poorest areas of Belgium, growing potatoes, heather and fir trees but little else. Canals, coal and proximity to the sea have helped cover this lonely moorland with great chemical and metallurgical plants that have transformed it within a decade. Nearby, no longer isolated, lies the small town of Mol, the centre of Belgium's atomic energy industry. When supplies of Congolese uranium were plentiful, Belgium hoped to share the lead in European production of nuclear energy, and set up an atomic centre even before the six-nation community, Euratom, was created in 1958. Nowadays chimney stacks, the vast dumpy cylinders of reactors and water-cooling towers dominate the once lonely landscape.

A few miles away from Mol lies the quiet little Flemish town of Geel, which centuries ago established an unusual skill that now is attracting attention among doctors and psychiatrists all over the world. At Geel, the mentally sick are cared for in the homes of local people, and live as normally as their condition allows. This practice was established as early as the fifteenth century; it began when pilgrims flocked to the tomb of a refugee Irish princess who was said to have cured her father's insanity by her own death. From the start these patients were treated in a humane and considerate way, in contrast to the brutality that medieval people usually showed to the insane. Nowadays, this 'home' treatment is of course supervised by specialists from the Geel mental hospital. The same pattern of treatment is being adopted in a few places elsewhere outside Belgium, but it appears to be particularly successful at Geel because of the local families' long experience of abnormal behaviour.

Travelling south from the lowland moors of the Campine, one enters the area of rolling wheatfields which stretches the whole width of the country through Hesbaye, Brabant and Hainaut. Between Liége and Namur, the river Meuse forms its natural southern boundary. East of Liége, around Eupen and Malmédy, lie the wild and beautiful uplands of the Hautes Fagnes. Here the people still speak the German they used before their area was handed over to Belgium after World War I. But this third language, spoken by about 60,000 'Walloons', has given Belgium little trouble. By now most people here are bilingual; children are taught both French and German at school, and can enrich themselves through fluency in two of Europe's leading languages.

Liége itself is Belgium's largest Walloon city, and the centre of the iron country that produced so much wealth during the nineteenth century. The Meuse valley forms a peaceful escape route for the citizens of Liége's industrial hinterland until, west of Namur, the Black Country rises between the Meuse and the Sambre. Mons, Charleroi, La Louvière, the home of Belgium's main coalmines, rival the Liége district in the size and number of their blast furnaces, steelworks and rolling mills, which fill the daytime air with noise and dust, and turn the night sky a Wagnerian red. This, more than any, is the area of mining disasters, of the explosive gaiety of the *ducasses*, of brass bands and pigeon racing: special weather details are broadcast every weekend for the pigeon-fancying *colombophiles*. It is through this area that the spectacular Tour de France bicycle race usually passes, exciting Belgians as much as Frenchmen. Since 1967, the area of Chièvres-Casteau, near Mons, has also been the seat of the Supreme Headquarters, Allied Powers in Europe (SHAPE) – the NATO organization evicted from its home in Paris by General de Gaulle and now quite well settled in this bleak but hospitable land.

South of the Black Country the terrain once more changes. The chalk soil makes relatively poor farming country but favours the profusion of wild daffodils that delights the local people and the season's first tourists every spring. In addition, quarries provide the stone with which almost all of Belgium's roads were paved until the present century – making the characteristic cobbled streets that are the bane of modern motorists. Farther south again, the land is wild; heath, broom, ferns and blueberries made this Ardennes region little valued until recently, except as a hunting ground for Belgian monarchs. Otherwise it was neglected until the first world war, when hungry Belgians became aware of its wealth of wild boar and other game. Nowadays, the lonely beauty of the area attracts innumerable tourists from the rest of small overcrowded Belgium and from farther afield.

In particular, the region around Bastogne near the Luxembourg border has become a place of American pilgrimage, to the graves of the United States soldiers and to the Bastogne Mardesson memorial commemorating the lives lost during the last Nazi offensive of December 1944. In that last desperate thrust, General von Rundstedt ordered every available German soldier who could speak English to be put into American uniform and sent to confuse advancing American troops. From the moment the US commanders discovered the ruse, any GI was likely to be suddenly asked: 'Where are you from? What's the capital of your state?'

Bastogne is only the latest of many Belgian towns that have been scenes of battle; most of Belgium has been fought over at some time in its history. Mons itself became a centre of British fighting during the first world war; and in Flanders, sad acres of small regimented crosses bear witness to the Allied dead. In Ypres, the Menin Gate was built as a memorial to the 55,000 British who died in World War I without any known grave.

BELGIANS ABROAD

Belgians complain about their climate, but don't leave home. This is the legend that has been current in Belgium ever since Leopold II complained he could not persuade his compatriots to go out and colonize the Congo or anywhere else. But like most such sayings, it is only partly accurate. True, Belgians make somewhat sick jokes about their *drache nationale* – the rain that falls so frequently as to be thought a national institution. It is also true that while Belgians join Northern Europe's annual migration in search of the sun, they remain passionately attached to their local neighbourhood – as they have been for centuries.

Yet it would be unjust to say that Belgians are unadventurous and reluctant to settle abroad. They are not more sedentary than other European peoples, but less has been heard of their foreign exploits than of those of their bigger neighbours. Few English people today know that, several centuries before the Christian era, Belgian tribes settled around the Winchester area of southern England, under a king Cunobeline who later became Shakespeare's Cymbeline; and that through the Middle Ages there was a constant influx of Flemings into East Anglia and the south-east coast regions – a trickle that became something of a tide during Belgium's turbulent fourteenth century, and again during the religious persecutions of two hundred years later.

Belgians claim with pride that their ancestors were in the vanguard of the early medieval Crusades. In particular, a nobleman from the Ardennes, Godfrey of Bouillon, became first Christian ruler of Jerusalem, and was succeeded in turn by his brother Baldwin of Hainaut. In 1204 another Baldwin, of Hainaut and Flanders, became first king of Constantinople. But eventually the combination of cupidity and religious fervour aroused by the Crusades found another outlet: the Flemish-born emperor Charles V chose many of his northern compatriots to help open up the sixteenth-century Spanish empire in the New World, and sent out Belgian missionaries as evangelists to follow the soldiers. A man of Bruges, Jean de Witte, became first bishop of Cuba; Peter of Ghent baptized three hundred thousand American Indians, and two Belgians, Josse Rycke and Pierre Gossens, discovered the Andes.

Religious troubles caused a different exodus after the abdication of Charles V, when his son Philip II intensified the repressive policies against non-Catholics. Apart from the mass escape of the middle classes, attracted by Protestantism, from the Spanish Inquisition to Holland, England or Germany, Walloon ironfounders from Liége settled in Sweden, and started the iron industry that flourishes there to this day. Others used their European refuges as jumping-off points for a new life in the New World.

One of these groups is said to have made history by founding New York – a claim that Belgians are now immensely proud to make, although at the time few in Europe cared what happened to the small obscure pioneering groups so far away. Belgian historians say the founders of New York were Protestant Walloons who had settled in the Dutch town of Leyden, in the hope of one day returning to their homeland; but when these hopes had dimmed, the children of the first emigrants took ship for North America, landing in the estuary of the Hudson River and leaving eight families on Manhattan Island, in a colony which they called New Avesnes after the Ardennes town of that name. Their first governor, Peter Minuit, bought the island in 1626 from the Manhattan Indians for about twenty-four dollars. It was then officially named Nova Belgica and only later, when its Dutch inhabitants had become predominant, did it come to be known as New Netherland. In 1924 a monument was unveiled on Manhattan Point in New York, commemorating the Walloon founders of the city.

From the seventeenth century onwards there were Belgians among the settlers, explorers, missionaries and merchants who gradually began to people the vast new continent. One of the most outstanding was Father Hennepin of Ath in Hainaut, who went to Canada in 1675 as a Franciscan missionary, and three years later joined the expedition of the French explorer Robert La Salle, bound for the mouth of the Mississippi. With a small group of companions Father Hennepin explored about one-third of the river. Later he wrote a *Description of Louisiana*, published in Paris, which attracted enormous interest and was translated into most European languages; it fired the imagination of contemporaries with its descriptions of America's size, its great rivers, its vast forests and wide plains. A later missionary, the Jesuit Father de Smedt, travelled thousands of miles through rough unexplored country in the north-west and far west. He too wrote about his experiences, including the peace he made with the great Indian chief Sitting Bull.

The records on Belgian immigration into the United States go back only to 1820, and show that there was a little-known, little-investigated influx of both Flemings and Walloons into the American melting pot throughout the nineteenth century, most of them driven by the economic tyranny that caused the working class to live on the edge of pauperism during this age of increasing middle-class affluence. After the Flemish potato famine of the 1840s, farmers and textile workers from Flanders entered the United States at the rate of about six to seven thousand a year. There was also a number of skilled emigrés from the coal, steel and glass industries of the Walloon areas. Altogether, Belgian immigration totalled about 104,000 between 1820 and 1910 and about 62,000 from 1910 to 1950; but when the modest quota of 1,350 was fixed for Belgium, it remained annually unfilled for many years. Detroit housed the largest Flemish colony, while Walloons settled in numbers in Wisconsin, particularly in Door County, whose villages and cemeteries have many names with a characteristic Walloon ring. Towns and villages across the continent bear Belgian names such as Liege, Charleroi, Ghent, Antwerp, Namur and Brussels, although it is difficult to determine with any certainty whether these indicate Belgian settlements.

Early in the nineteenth century Belgium played a small but unexpected role in American history, in that the city of Ghent was the scene of peace negotiations almost throughout the strange war that flickered rather than flared between Great Britain and the United States between 1812 and 1814. Disputes at sea and a quarrel over Canadian boundaries led President James Madison to declare war on Britain – just at the moment when the United States Ambassador in London had secured a repeal of most of the measures that had led to friction. Understandably, the British wanted peace with America so as to concentrate their efforts against Napoleon; but in the days before wireless telegraphy it was too late to call the war off. After some US successes, the British sailed up Chesapeake Bay and took Washington itself, so suddenly that British officers finished off the dinner of the fleeing President Madison while it and the battle were still hot. Attempts to seize Baltimore ended in failure; in any case both sides had set up peace-making machinery in Ghent as soon as war broke out. John Quincy Adams resided in that city as head of the American negotiating team until peace was finally signed on 24 December 1814; the two teams ate their Christmas meal together the next day.

Belgium played an important role for the United States in a later, bigger war in which America and her allies were racing to invent the weapon that would, it was hoped, put an end to all wars. Shortly before Belgium was invaded in May 1940, Edgar Sengier, managing director of the Union Minière of Katanga, ordered all uranium ore at the company's plant near Antwerp to be shipped for safety to the United States. Later in the same year, when the victorious Nazi armies were pushing down from North Africa, Sengier also got all the available uranium ore removed from the Congolese mine at Shinkolobwe. Over a thousand tons of it were stacked in steel drums near the dock on Staten Island and stayed there unguarded and unnoticed for two years, until General Leslie R. Groves, chief of the atomic weapon project, heard of it and bought it. Apart from its quantity, the quality of the ore was far superior to that from Canada or Colorado on which work had so far depended; the Allies no longer needed to fear running out of the basic material. For his wartime help, Edgar Sengier was awarded the Medal of Merit by the United States government, the first non-American to receive it.

Of all Belgium's modern writers, Georges Simenon has the widest international reputation. Born in 1903 in Liége, he brilliantly described the atmosphere of his native Belgium in his earlier stories, which he began to write soon after he began work at the age of sixteen as a journalist on the *Gazette de Liége*. Later he left Belgium for America and Switzerland, and has now published over two hundred novels, earning himself the praise of Gide and Mauriac as the Balzac of the detective story.

The key to his early success was the quick recognition he won in Paris. Such are the economics of publishing that it is virtually impossible for a Belgian French-language writer to make either a name or an income for himself unless his work is accepted by one of the big Paris publishers. Usually, indeed, Belgium first takes notice of her own new authors if their work is sold at home in a Parisian edition. From Paris, a writer has a potential readership of about 220 millions, whereas Belgium alone could offer only about five million; few Belgian publishing houses except the Marabout Université of Verviers have strong enough international links to push their wares effectively through the French-speaking world.

Flemish authors have an even more difficult time and depend even more than French-language writers on government subsidies. They can tap a linguistic community of only about twenty millions, including the Netherlands and South Africa. Despite Flanders' great efforts to foster Flemish culture, the Flemings do not buy books as readily as do the Dutch, and it is an advantage to Flemish authors to be published in Holland by a Dutch firm. But for Flemish as for Dutch writers, translation is essential if they are to break through to a wider audience – and in translation they risk the loss of their writing's peculiar strength.

Like Simenon, Félicien Marceau, who won the Goncourt Prize in December 1969, left his native land early in his career. He settled in France soon after the second world war. His prizewinning novel, *Creezy*, is a modishly doomed story of a French parliamentarian's passion for a model girl who lives in a world of high fashion, fast cars and transient love. Earlier, Marceau had already made a name for himself in France with popular boulevard plays such as *L'Oeuf* ('The Egg') and *La Bonne Soupe*. Before him, French-language writer Charles Plisnier had found success both in Belgium and beyond. His *False Passports* won the Goncourt Prize in 1936 with its story of latent revolution in Europe between the wars. Françoise Mallet-Joris is a prolific novelist whose *Empire Céleste* brought her the Femina Prize in 1958. Beatrice Beck won the Goncourt in 1952 for her *Leon Morn the Priest*: in the same year Dominique Rolin won the Femina Prize for her novel *Breath*, while Francis Walder won the Goncourt prize in 1958 with his *Negotiation*. These writers stand out as having earned the accolade of Paris, but others who are also talented though somewhat less well-known include Marie Gevers, Marcel Thiry, Liliane Wouters, Andrée Sodenkamp, Charles Bertin and Georges Sion. The critical works of Lucien Christophe, of Marcel Lobet and of Paul Haesaerts, and the historical writings of Jacques Pirenne, son of the famous historian Henri Pirenne, also contribute to the reputation of contemporary Belgian writing in the French language. Finally, a word is due to that remarkable children's classic, the *Tintin* series of Hergé, known and loved by children all over the French-speaking world.

Felix Timmermans for many years held the leading place among twentieth-century Flemish novelists; like many of his compatriots his work was greatly influenced in subject-matter and style by Flanders' Golden Age, as in his *Peasants' Psalm*, the *Beautiful Hours of the Lady Symphorose*, and *Pallieter*. His contemporary Gerard Walschap had a more obsessively tragic view of life; his *Roothooft Family* shows the Flemish peasant as victim of inexorable destiny; and Gaston Duribreux gives a similarly dour portrait of North Sea fishermen. Jan-Albert Goris, who is also a poet and critic, won renown with his novel *Joachim of Babylon*. Piet van Aken, Prosper de Smet, Yvo Michiels, Hubert Lampo and Paul Lebeau have also published notable work, while Johan Daisne specializes in dreamy, sometimes macabre fantasies. Jos Vandeloo made a name for himself in the 1950s with his *Playful Parade* and *The Wall*; while Hugo Claus's *Duck Shoot* and *The Cold Lover* show his talents as a novelist, though it is in the theatre that he has chiefly made his name.

The theatre in Belgium received little attention until long after the revival of Flemish and French literature in the nineteenth century. It was Maurice Maeterlinck who revolutionized the Belgian theatre with his *Blue Bird* and *Pelleas and Melisande*; significantly, he also first found success in Paris. After him Fernand Crommelynck achieved fame both in France and Belgium during the 1920s with his explosive and tormented *Magnificent Cuckold* and *The Woman whose Heart is too Small*; while Michel de Ghelderode, who died in 1962, was one of the many French-speaking Flemings who turned to the Middle Ages for his inspiration. He had almost reached the end of his life before his mystery plays, such as *Escurial* and *Barabbas*, received due recognition. More recently, Edmond Kinds gained wide favour with his *Sparrows of Baltimore*, and José André Lacour's *Examination Year* has amused audiences both in Brussels and Paris.

The Flemish-language theatre was dominated for much of the present century by Herman Tierlinck with his open-air pageants and his plays such as *I Serve* and *The Magpie on the Gallows*. Other writers of popular and successful plays were Willem Putman, Paul de Mont and Herwig Hensen; the leader of the younger generation has been Hugo Claus, particularly known for his *Bride in the Morning*; his best-known contemporaries are Jozel Van Hoeck and Tone Brulin, though other younger writers are emerging, with the present upsurge of pride in Flemish culture.

Since 1951 theatres have received regular financial support from the government. The Flemings have three subsidized theatres: the Koninklijke Vlaamse Schouwburg of Brussels, the National Toneel of Ghent and the Koninklijke Nederlandse Schouwburg in Antwerp. The three French-language theatres on the other hand are all in Brussels; the National Theatre aims more than the other two at popular education and claims kinship with the Théâtre National Populaire of Paris, while the Royal Park Theatre has a literary repertory rather similar to that of the Comédie Française, and the Brussels Curtain Theatre tries out new, *avant-garde* works. Only the National Theatre takes its productions into the provinces (where Liége, in particular, has a flourishing theatrical tradition). Another Brussels theatre, the Royal Monnaie, is outstanding for its Ballets of the Twentieth Century; under its French choreographer Maurice Béjart, the Monnaie theatre company has won a reputation for brilliant experiments in modern dance. In music, both vocal and orchestral, Flanders is more active and lively than the Walloon provinces, although both benefit from the excellent Belgian Conservatoire. Regrettably, Belgian radio and television do not exploit the opportunity that both ballet and music would seem to offer to give joint programmes. The outstanding annual musical event is the international Queen Elisabeth competition founded by King Baudouin's grandmother in 1951; it attracts young soloists from all over the world. Belgians have not often won its first prizes, though Arthur Grumiaux of the Belgian Conservatoire has won an international reputation as a violinist.

Recent painting, in Belgium as elsewhere, has been marked by the vogue for abstract art. Anne Bonnet, Gaston Bertrand, Louis Van Lint, Marc Mendelson, Jean Milo and Joe Delahaut have produced widely-praised work, but the greatest Belgian painters of the twentieth century are undoubtedly the Surrealists René Magritte and Paul Delvaux. Magritte painted in a style that varied little until his death in August 1967 in Brussels since he formed it in the 1920s; he was faithful to the surrealist principle of taking common objects out of their context and putting them into new, improbable or unnatural settings – one of his favourite and characteristic images, for example, was the man whose chest is replaced by a cage of birds. Delvaux's typical themes are semi-draped or nude women together with fully-clothed twentieth-century men in a dreamlike décor of Renaissance architecture. In the sense that the fantastic can and does at any time irrupt into settings that are minutely realistic, the work of both painters shows their links with medieval Flemish art.

Belgian cinema has a long history, beginning as far back as 1834 with Joseph Plateau's fast-moving disc, the Phenakistiscope, that marked a great step forward in the pioneering of moving images. Before the first world war Belgium had produced some feature-length films, but later became outstanding in the production of documentaries of high quality such as Henri Storck's *World of Paul Delvaux*; with Paul Haesaerts, Storck made *Rubens* and *The Open*

Window, the latter a survey of landscape painting from the Flemish primitives to the French impressionists. In turn Paul Haesarts made *The Golden Age*, a beautiful and elaborate panorama of the Flemish primitives from Van Eyck to Brueghel, the well-known *Visit to Picasso* and more recently, *Brueghel*. Among the Belgian talent that moved to France, Charles Spaak became a leading script-writer, noted for the *Kermesse Héroïque* made by Belgian-born Jacques Feyder, while actors such as Fernand Gravey, Fernand Ledoux, Catherine Spaak – as well as singers Jacques Brel and Annie Cordy – were considered to be French. Only recently have Belgians again launched out on full-length films: Paul Meyer made a long documentary on the Borinage miners in 1960, while Emile Degelin's *If the Wind Frightens You* was not well received despite some excellent camera work on location among the sand dunes of Belgium's North Sea Coast. André Delvaux's *Man who Had his Hair Cut Short*, adapted from the Flemish novel by Johan Daisne, has enjoyed, like the novel itself, much critical success.

UNION MAKES STRENGTH

This brief study of the arts shows that, culturally, Belgium belongs to two worlds. The creation of two separate Ministries of Culture in 1968 has emphasized a long-standing tendency for the two linguistic groups to go their separate ways.

For the French-speaking Belgian the natural pole of attraction is France. This results in a talent drain which tends to leave many Belgians feeling culturally impoverished. The Netherlands are less of a magnet to Flemings, although the two Dutch-speaking regions are now far closer to each other than in earlier days when Dutchmen tended (as some still do) to consider their southern neighbours as culturally poor relations.[2] Soon after the second world war Holland and the Flemish-speaking provinces decided to restore the cultural unity they shared until the sixteenth century. Flemings now discuss literary output, publishing, radio and television in regular meetings with their Dutch co-linguists far more than with their own compatriots. The same is largely true of the Walloons and the French. Not so long ago Walloon dialects were more common in the south of

Belgium than French. Today, with their backs to the wall economically, Walloons use the French language as one of their main assets. They speak standard French, with a heavy accent, and its use gives them a feeling of cultural superiority. Though they may love France, however, they are not always greatly loved in return. Writers such as Baudelaire, Verlaine, Rimbaud and Taine have written scathingly about Belgium and have set the tone for a common French attitude that is wounding to Walloons' self-esteem.

Some Belgians deplore the cultural division and believe that it is another powerful force which weakens the country's claim to be considered a valid political entity. Belgium was created as an independent state a century and a half ago by European powers who undoubtedly acted for reasons of policy unconnected with any human considerations. General de Gaulle has always maintained that Belgium is not and cannot be a nation. Yet he and others who tend to share his views overlook the fact that something like the present Belgian state had already existed for centuries before 1830. In the nineteenth century and even earlier, broadly speaking, the Walloon south became the home of heavy industries and sold its goods to the agricultural, populous north in exchange for food and manpower.

As we have seen, Flanders is now rapidly industrializing while the older Walloon industries are in difficulty, so that the two halves of the country now tend to rival more than to complement each other. Furthermore, it is argued, as the European Common Market brings down national barriers, Belgium will tend less than ever to exist as a separate economic entity; in trade at least, each half of the country would be able to link itself with different Common Market neighbours across the vanished frontiers.

If, therefore, Belgium does not form a unit either culturally, economically or geographically; if, politically, domestic issues seem to be splitting the country apart, what cement can be strong enough to hold it together? The monarchy, perhaps. King Baudouin has been remarkably successful in avoiding his father's error of becoming identified with only one half of the country; but critics who take a longer view point out that until 1830 the Saxe-Coburg house had no roots whatsoever in Belgium. It might seem, therefore, that nowadays Belgium has no compelling reason to stay united. Some federalists look forward to the day when Belgium might dissolve within the looser amalgam of a uniting Europe.

Yet Europe is proving as slow to unite as Belgium is slow to fall apart. It seems much more likely that Belgium will continue into the future as an entity with some kind of internal federal structure. After more than a century together, the two halves of the country may lack a cement to hold them, but none the less have a complex web of enmeshed material interests, whose power to bind should not be underestimated. The sentiment of a common national interest would still probably hold if the alternative seriously threatened the citizens' living standards, or undermined the value of the Belgian franc. In the end such down-to-earth considerations would probably keep both partners together, however restlessly. Like spouses in many a long-lasting marriage, each would risk too much by being left alone. There is still profound truth in the country's double national motto: *Eendracht maakt macht – L'Union fait la force*.

Nor would either half of the country care to risk being swallowed up by its co-linguist neighbours, if only because the independent spirit that makes them quarrel with each other causes them also to fear being restricted in their freedom by anyone else. Therefore although logically, in this age of bigger units, the Flemish area should join with Holland and Wallonia with France, Belgians have little enthusiasm for this solution. And whatever France might think about adopting the Walloons, the Protestants of the Netherlands, with over five million Catholics already on Dutch soil, would by no means care to have this number doubled.

Even some form of federalism or confederalism would bring no easy solution. Yet in its endless search for some form of regionalism, Belgium pinpoints in more ways than one a major problem of modern society: how to give antagonistic groups their just due, no more and no less. In these days of mass anonymity, it is significant and deeply understandable that men cling to inherited patterns that give them roots, and seek for solidarity with a group within which they can still feel themselves to be individuals, man-size. A solution for Belgium could be a solution for the world.

Notes on the text

2 RELIGION AND DIVISION

1 E. Alberi, *Le Relazioni degli Ambasciatori Veneti al Senato*, Ser. I, Vol. III (1853), p. 357.
2 R. H. Tawney, *Religion and the Rise of Capitalism* (London, 1936), p. 72.

3 PEOPLE INTO NATION

1 Frans van Kalken, *Histoire du peuple belge des origines à nos jours* (Brussels, 1949), p. 145.
2 'Sacred love of the motherland, give us back our daring and our pride.'

4 THE KINGDOM MEANS BUSINESS

1 A marriage had been arranged between William and Princess Charlotte of England, but Charlotte had refused to go through with it after meeting Leopold.
2 Letters exchanged between King Leopold and Queen Victoria on 9 and 19 April 1839.
3 The accusation against Captain Dreyfus, which led to the famous trial that shook France in the 1890s, was that he had revealed the secret French intention to capture these Meuse valley forts.
4 Comte Woeste, *Mémoires pour servir à l'histoire contemporaine de la Belgique* (Brussels, 1927), Vol. I, p. 149.
5 'It's paradise for capitalists and hell for the working classes' was his comment on Belgium.
6 Henri de Man and Louis de Brouckère, *Le Mouvement ouvrier en Belgique* (Brussels, 1965), pp. 39 and 64.
7 N. Pevsner, *Pioneers of Modern Design* (London, 1948), p. 229, note 20.

5 WARS AND LANGUAGES

1 F. Fischer, *Germany's Aims in the First World War* (London, 1967), pp. 111–13.

2 G. W. T. Omond, *The Kingdom of Belgium and the Grand Duchy of Luxembourg* (London, 1924), p. 149.

3 E. Cammaerts, *Albert of Belgium* (London, 1935), p. 376.

4 G. H. Dumont, *Léopold III, Roi des Belges* (Brussels, 1944), p. 241.

6 THE KING AND THE EXILES

1 According to the historian William Shirer, Hitler ordered this because he did not want the decisive battle, with inevitable civilian damage and casualties, to take place on Flemish territory; he had promised his Flemish supporters to set up an independent Flemish region, closely linked to Germany. *The Rise and Fall of the Third Reich* (Crest Books, New York, 1962), p. 966.

2 Winston Churchill, *The Second World War*, Vol. III: *The Fall of France* (Cassell paperback edition, London, 1964), p. 89.

3 Henri Michel, *Les Mouvements clandestines en Europe* (P.U.F., Paris, 1961). See also the *Guardian*, London, 1 September 1969, p. 9.

8 THE CONGO

1 Jo Gérard, *La Monarchie belge abandonnera-t-elle le Congo?* (Brussels, 1960), pp. 12–43.

2 R. S. Thomson, *Fondation de l'état indépendant du Congo* (Brussels, 1933), p. 30.

3 Quoted by J. Stengers in *Textes inédites d'Emile Banning* (Brussels, 1955), p. 13.

4 'It takes some time to drill and discipline a body of raw negroes; it generally takes a year. Punishment must be in two forms only – the stick or whip, or irons . . . the first is repulsive . . . if corporal punishment is excessive you also place the man on the sick list and thus rob yourself of his services. The best punishment is that of irons.' Stanley to the Comité d'Etudes, quoted by G. Martelli in *Leopold to Lumumba* (London, 1962), p. 65.

5 The missionary author of *Thinking Black* (London, 1912).

6 F. Cattier, *Etude sur la situation de l'état indépendant du Congo* (Brussels, 1906), pp. 74–5.

7 The Abako began as a cultural organization to spread the Kikongo language, but soon became a militant political party aiming at the ultimate

restoration of the ancient kingdom of the Bakongo in an area round the mouth of the Congo long divided between Belgium, Portugal and France.
8 A tract of the Mouvement National Congolais explained: 'Independence means total equality between blacks and whites. . . . If you must travel by foot to go somewhere, and happen to meet a European who drives a car, he must stop and pick you up . . . otherwise do not hesitate to take down the licence plate number . . . The European will be forced to go back to Europe, for he is an enemy of the Congolese.'
9 Paul-Henri Spaak, *Combats inachevés* (Paris, 1969), pp. 298–314.

9 FLEMINGS, WALLOONS AND OTHER WORRIES
1 Etienne-Charles Dayez, *La Belgique est-elle morte?* (Paris, 1969), p. 98.
2 For this the Terneuzen canal, which passes through Dutch territory, is being widened and deepened. The new plant, Sidmar, is owned by a consortium of Belgian, French, Italian and Luxembourg firms.
3 *Common Market*, Vol. 9, No. 6 (The Hague, June 1969), p. 124.
4 Carl-Hendrick Hojer: *Le Régime parlementaire belge de 1918 à 1940*, Uppsala, 1946, quoted in Dayez, *op. cit.*, p. 19.

10 BUSINESS, CHURCH AND STATE
1 Report in the *Economist* (London), 28 October 1961.

11 CULTURE, COUNTRYSIDE AND THE AMERICAN CONNECTION
1 Comte Louis de Lichtervelde, *Aspects de la Société Belge* (Brussels, 1958), p. 314.
2 *Memo from Belgium* No. 102 (Brussels, July 1968), p. 25.

Select Bibliography

Annual Reports of the European Coal and Steel Community, Luxembourg, and of the European Economic Community, Brussels.

Annual Economic Surveys of the Belgium-Luxembourg Economic Union by the Organization for Economic Co-operation and Development, Paris.

Arango, E. R., *Leopold III and the Belgian Royal Question*, Baltimore, 1961.

Asherson, N., *The King Incorporated*, London, 1963.

Belgian Ministry of Foreign Affairs, *The Official Account of What Happened 1939–40*, London, 1941.

Bibliothèque de l'Institut Belge de Science Politique, *Aspects de la Société Belge*, Brussels, 1958.

Brandi, K., *The Emperor Charles V*, London, 1939.

Bronne, C., *Leopold I et son Temps*, Brussels, 1947.

Cambridge Economic History of Europe, Vol. VI: *The Industrial Revolutions and After*, Cambridge, 1965.

Cammaerts, E., *Albert of Belgium*, London, 1935; *The Prisoner at Laeken*, London, 1941.

Chardonnet, J., *Les Grandes Puissances: Etude Economique*, Tome I, Paris, 1960.

Charriaut, H., *La Belgique Moderne, Terre d'Experiences*, Paris, 1910.

Chlepner, B. S., *Cen Ans d'Histoire Sociale en Belgique*, Brussels, 1958.

Cole, G. D. H., *A History of Socialist Thought*, Vol. V, *Socialism and Fascism*, London, 1960.

D'Alia, A., *La Belgique Intellectuelle, Economique, Politique*, Brussels, 1923.

Daye, P., *Leopold, II*, Paris, 1934.

Delsinne, A., *Le Parti Ouvrier Belge*, Brussels, 1955.

Dhondt, J., *Histoire de la Belgique*, Paris, 1963.

Dumont, G. H., *Leopold III, Roi des Belges*, Brussels, 1944.

Froude, J. A., *The Life and Letters of Erasmus*, London, 1899.

Granick, D., *The European Executive*, New York, 1964.

Huizinga, J. H., *Mr. Europe: a Political Biography of Paul-Henri Spaak*, London, 1961.

Joye, P., *Les Trusts en Belgique*, Brussels, 1961.

Lamfalussy, A., *Investment and Growth in Mature Economies: the Case of Belgium*, London, 1961.

Mallinson, V., *Power and Politics in Belgian Education 1815–1960*, London, 1963.

de Meeus, A., *Histoire des Belges*, Paris, 1958.

Motley, J. L., *The Rise of the Dutch Republic*, London, 1906.

Murray, P. and L., *The Art of the Renaissance*, London, 1963.

Noville, J., *Paul van Zeeland au Service de son Temps*, Brussels, 1954.

Page, J., *Leopold III*, London, n.d. (1959).

Pirenne, H., *Histoire de la Belgique*, 8 vols, Brussels, 1932.

Proudfoot, M. J., *European Refugees: a Study in Forced Population Movement*, London, 1957.

juapport présenté par la Commission d'Information établie par le Roi le 14 Rillet 1946.

Rapport présenté par le Sécrétariat du Roi sur les événements politiques qui ont suivi la libération, mai 1945–oct 1949.

Receuil de Documents établi par le Sécrétariat du Roi concernant la période 1963–49.

Rowntree, S., *Land and Labour; Lessons from Belgium*, London, 1911.

Sayers, R. S. (ed.), *Banking in Western Europe*, Oxford, 1962.

Schreiber, M., *Belgium*, London, 1945.

Supplément au Receuil de Documents établi par le Sécrétariat du Roi concernant la période 1936–50.

Vaussard, M., *Histoire de la Démocratie Chrétienne*, Paris, 1956.

Whitlock, B., *Belgium under German Occupation*, London, 1918.

Anstey, R. T., *Britain and the Congo in the 19th Century*, Oxford, 1962.

Davister, P., *Katanga, Enjeu du Monde*, Brussels, 1960.

Inforcongo, *Belgian Congo*, 2 vols., Brussels, 1960.

Institut Royal des Relations Internationales, *La Crise Congolaise*, Brussels, 1960; *Evolution de la Crise Congolaise*, Brussels, 1961.

Joye, P. and Lewin, R., *Les Trusts au Congo*, Brussels, 1961.

Lemarchand, R., *Political Awakening in the Congo*, Berkeley and Los Angeles, 1964.

Martelli, G., *Leopold to Lumumba*, London, 1962.
Oliver, R. and Fage, J. D., *A Short History of Africa*, London, 1962.
Slade, R., *The Belgian Congo, Some Recent Changes*, Oxford, 1960.
Slade, R., *King Leopold's Congo*, London, 1962.

Acknowledgments

ACEC, 22; Associated Press, 15; Jerry Bauer, 17; Belgian State Tourist Office, 1, 2; Bibliothèque Royale de Belgique, 6, 7; by courtesy of the Trustees of the British Museum, 4; Camera Press, 18; Suzy Gablik, 19; Jacques Halber, 28; Institut Belge d'Information et de Documentation, 8, 10, 14, 16, 20, 23–27; Keystone, 21; Musée des Beaux Arts, Brussels, 5; Musée Royal de l'Afrique Centrale, Terveuren, 12; Radio Times Hulton Picture Library, 11; Thames and Hudson archives, 3, 9; L'Union Minière de Haut Katanga, 13.

ANSEELE, EDOUARD. A pioneer of the Flemish socialist movement, founder of the immensely successful Voruit cooperative movement, and co-founder with César de Paepe (*q.v.*) of the Belgian Workers' Party in 1885. By trade a typographer, Anselle became a deputy for Ghent in 1894. He founded the Belgian Workers' Bank in 1913. Died in 1938.

ANTO-CARTE. A Brussels artist born in Mons in 1886. Painter of sturdy though idealized Belgian folk figures, he celebrated the solid peasant virtues of hard work and the simple life.

BAEKELAND, LEO H. The inventor of bakelite, to which he gave his name. He left his home town Ghent in 1889 after studying physics and chemistry at Ghent university; settled in the United States and died there in 1944.

COPPÉ, ALBERT. Vice-president of the High Authority of the European Coal and Steel Community since its inception in 1952, Albert Coppé was appointed one of the fourteen members of the single joint commission of the European Communities in Brussels in July 1967, and one of the nine members of the new commission that took office in July 1970. A graduate of Louvain University, he held three ministries in the early 1950s as a member of the Christian Social Party.

DE BROUCKÈRE, LOUIS. A leader of the Socialist movement and, from 1922 to 1930, Belgian representative at the League of Nations. Died in 1952. Brussels' Times Square or Piccadilly Circus, the Place de Brouckère, is named after him.

DE BRUYNE, HENRI. A hero of the anti-slavery wars in the Congo, De Bruyne refused to abandon his chief who was lying ill, when offered a chance to escape from Arab leaders. He died in September 1892.

DE GERLACHE DE GOMERY, ADRIEN. Organized first polar expedition to spend winter in Antarctic, in 1897, and discovered two islands that he named Antwerp and Brabant. His son Gaston led another expedition to the same area in 1957–58.

DE MAN, HENRI. Author of 'Beyond Marxism', advocating the abandonment of the theory of the class struggle. He also outlined a Labour Plan, which was adopted by the British Labour Party and the Trade Union Congress in the 1930s, featuring a mixed economy of socialism and capitalism. Became president of the Belgian Workers' Party in 1939, but dissolved it when Belgium was invaded during the following year. Was not a Nazi, but believed in Nazi victory. Escaped to Switzerland in 1942, was repudiated by his party after the war, and died in exile in 1952.

DE PAEPE, CÉSAR. One of leading thinkers of international Socialist movement and an outstanding member of first Socialist International. Later helped create the Brabant Workers' Party, which fused with the Flemish socialist movement to form first Workers' party of all Belgium in 1885. Died in 1890.

DHANIS, BARON. A leader of the forces of King Leopold II's Congo in successful wars against Arab slave-traders, from 1891 to 1894.

DOUCY, ARTHUR. Director of the Solvay Sociology Institute of Brussels University. Doucy proposed a plan for decentralization of Belgian government administration in the Congo, which was much discussed in 1957; it advocated a royal commissioner for each Congolese province, a plan that was found particularly attractive by the Katangese.

ELISABETH, third Queen of the Belgians, who died in 1965 at the age of eighty-nine, had been throughout her life a leading figure of Belgium's cultural life and counted among her friends David Oistrakh, Albert Einstein and Jean Cocteau. Late in life she travelled in the Soviet Union and in Communist China; her left-wing sympathies were tolerated with indulgent affection by most Belgians. In 1951 she created the music contest for young artists that has now become internationally famous.

FAYAT, HENRI. Socialist member of the Belgian Chamber of Representatives, and Minister for European Affairs in the Lefèvre-Spaak government of 1961–65, with special emphasis on work of Common Market. Born in Molenbeek, Brussels in 1908, Fayat volunteered for free Belgian forces in London in 1942, and held many political offices, including Ministry of Commerce from May 1957 to June 1958.

GRÉTRY, ANDRÉ MODESTE. A musician of Liége who later also studied in Rome, he wrote outstandingly successful light operas. Died in 1913 in Paris.

HARMEL, PIERRE. Prime Minister from July 1965 to March 1966, and Minister of Foreign Affairs in the following Catholic–Liberal coalition. President of Walloon wing of Christian Social party, and first director of Harmel Centre for the study of Flemish and Walloon problems – on which he made a major report in 1958. Born 1911 in Brussels.

HYMANS, PAUL. President of first General Assembly of the League of Nations, and Liberal minister in several coalition cabinets during the early years of this century.

JANSON, MARIE. Daughter of the nineteenth-century progressive Liberal and mother of Paul-Henri Spaak, she was the first woman to enter parliament when the Socialist party elected her to the Senate in 1922.

LEFÈVRE, THÉODORE A. M. Prime Minister from 1961 to 1965 in the Catholic–Socialist coalition which had Paul-Henri Spaak as vice-premier and Foreign Minister. President from 1950 to 1961 of the Christian Social Party and from 1960 to 1966 of the International Union of Christian Democrats. Born in 1914 at Ghent.

MAX, ADOLPHE. Became a national hero after he had refused to co-operate with the occupying authorities when burgomaster of Brussels early in 1914. Was imprisoned throughout the four years of World War I.

MERTENS DE WILMARS, JOSEPH M. H. C. Appointed judge of the Court of Justice of the European Communities at Luxembourg on 7 October 1967. Author of works on public and administrative law as well as on European law. Member of Belgian Chamber of Representatives from 1952 to 1962. Born at St Niklaas Waas in 1912.

PERMEKE, CONSTANT. Antwerp painter who died in 1952. Painted evocative landscapes – some of them fron the English countryside where he convalesced from war wounds during World War I – and also sombre stylized figures drawn from Belgian life.

PIRENNE, HENRI. Author of a monumental history of Belgium, which is acknowledged as a European classic. Died in 1935.

PLANTIN, CHRISTOPHER. Originated a type that still bears his name, but is best known for his printing of the polyglot bible published in Antwerp during the years 1569–73.

REY, JEAN. From 1967 to 1970 was first president of the joint commission of the European communities, after having been one of nine members of the Common Market commission since 1958. Liberal deputy for Liége for many years, and Minister of Economic Affairs in the 1954–58 Liberal–Socialist coalition government. Born in Liége, the son of a Protestant pastor, in 1902.

RUBENS, PETER PAUL. Internationally-known painter; but also diplomat of the court of the seventeenth-century Archdukes Albert and Isabella. Was entrusted with many delicate diplomatic missions, including several to London to foster the reconciliation of England and Spain.

SAX, ADOLPHE. A Dinant musician who invented the saxophone in 1846.

SLUTER, CLAUS. A fifteenth-century sculptor, famous for the doorway and the Moses fountain of the Carthusian monastery of Champmol at Dijon.

SPAAK, PAUL-HENRI. Belgium's best-known living statesman. Held public office for almost thirty-five years, often as Belgium's Foreign Minister. Was first president of the General Assembly of the United Nations, and first chairman of the Consultative Assembly of the Council of Europe. Left public life and the Socialist party in July 1966 after the fall of the Harmel government (in which he had been Foreign Minister); then took up a career in an international business corporation. Born at Brussels in 1899.

STRUYE, PAUL. President of the Belgian Senate, a leading member of the Christian Social Party and writer of a regular weekly political column in the daily *La Libre Belgique*.

VAN ACKER, ACHILLE. President of the Belgian Chamber of Representatives and active in Socialist parliamentary politics during most of his life (born in 1898 at Bruges). First premier after World War II and one of leaders of Socialist opposition to King Leopold III.

VANDEN BOEYNANTS, PAUL. Premier from March 1966 to 1968, as leader of a Catholic–Liberal coalition; early in 1967 launched an austerity programme very similar to the 1966–67 British 'squeeze'. Born in Brussels in 1919. Bilingual in Flemish and French, he played a prominent part in the long controversy over the statute for Brussels.

VAN ZEELAND, PAUL, VISCOUNT. First became prominent in Belgian public life in the 1930s, when he reformed the banking and credit structure of the country during the depression years; held office as Premier and Foreign Minister in a series of post-war governments, but returned to his banking career. Is a founder-member of the Atlantic Institute, created in 1957, and has been associated with all the principal moves towards creating a united Europe in friendship with the United States. Was born in 1893. A graduate of Princeton University and of the University of Louvain.

WOUTERS, RIK. Flemish painter and sculptor who died in 1916. He was noted for solid-looking bronzes, and for the vigorous canvases which added a peculiarly Belgian coda to the Impressionist movement.

Index

Numbers in italic refer to illustrations

Mertens de Wilmars, Joseph (*see*
  Who's Who, p. 193)
Metsys, Quentin, 27
Meuse, 11, 34, 41, 63, 171
Meyer, Paul, 181
Minuit, Peter, 174
missionaries, 107, 108, 117
Mobutu, Joseph, 118–19
More, Sir Thomas, 27
Morel, E. D., 108
Mouvement national belge, 88
Mouvement national congolais, 114
Mouvement populaire wallon, 155
Murat, Joachim, 44
Murphy, J. B., 108

NAPOLEON, 37
Napoleon III, 49
National Congress (1830), 40–1
national dishes, 165–6
NATO, 10, 95, 128–9, 139, 140, 158–9
Nemours, Duke of, 41
Netherlands, Kingdom of the, 38
New York, founding of, 174
novelists, Belgian, 177–8

'ONS LAND', 160
Organization for European Economic
  Co-operation (OEEC), 95
Ortelius, Abraham, 27, *74*
Ostend Company, 33
Oudenaarde, 19, 33

PAINTING, 180; Flemish, 19–20
Palmerston, Lord, 40, 41, 42, 44
Pan, 160
parliament, 45–6, 63, 157–8; *see also*
  Estates General

Parti Ouvrier Belge, 53, 54, 154
Parti Social Chrétien, 93–4, 97, 100
Party of Liberty and Progress, 132, 155–6
Peasants' League, 55, 153
Pepin the Short, 12
Permeke, Constant (*see* Who's Who,
  p. 194)
Peter of Ghent, 174
Petit, Gabrielle, 61
Petrus Christus, 19
Philip II, 28 *ff.*
Philip, Archduke, 25
Philip, Duke, 18, 21
Philippe le Bel, 16
Pierlot, Hubert, 72, 84, 86, 91
Pire, Fr Georges, 162
Pirenne, Henri (*see* Who's Who,
  p. 194)
Piron Brigade, 90
Plantin, Christophe (*see* Who's Who,
  p. 194), 27, *74*
Plisnier, Charles, 178
polder land, 11, 34, *146*, 170;
  draining of, 15
political parties, 153–6, 162–4
population problems, 127
Pottier, Abbé, 55
Pourquoi Pas, 160
Press, the, 159–60
processions and festivals, 18, 32, 35,
  76, *148*, 168–9
Protestantism, 27
publishing, economics of, 177

RASSEMBLEMENT WALLON, 132, 156
Renkin, Jules, 55
Republic of the United States of
  Belgium, proclamation of the, 35–6
Requesens, Luis de, 29
resources, natural, 11
revolution (1830), 39–40